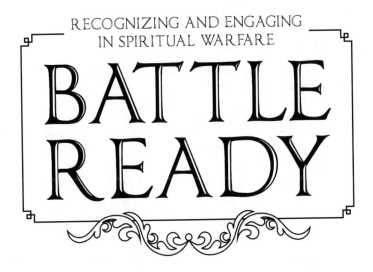

RECOGNIZING AND ENGAGING
IN SPIRITUAL WARFARE

BATTLE READY

MIKE MAYHUGH

WestBow
PRESS®
A DIVISION OF THOMAS NELSON
& ZONDERVAN

Disclaimer by author:
Some of the anecdotal illustrations in this book are true to life and are included with the permission of the person named. All other illustrations are composites of real situations from a variety of pastoral sources, and any resemblance to people living or dead is coincidental.

WestBow Press books may be ordered through booksellers or by contacting:

WestBow Press
A Division of Thomas Nelson & Zondervan
1663 Liberty Drive
Bloomington, IN 47403
www.westbowpress.com
1 (866) 928-1240

ISBN: 978-1-5127-3556-7 (sc)
ISBN: 978-1-5127-3557-4 (hc)
ISBN: 978-1-5127-3555-0 (e)

Library of Congress Control Number: 2016904914

Print information available on the last page.

WestBow Press rev. date: 04/12/2016

CONTENTS

DEDICATION

To my loving wife, Lisa, my hero, who is one of the best warriors I have ever known. I do not know where I would be today without her always standing in the gap for me. After Jesus, she is God's greatest gift to me!

FOREWORD

"When Augustine equates the Kingdom of God with the church and the kingdom of Satan with the great world empires, he is partly right and partly wrong. He is right in asserting that in principle the church is the representative of the Kingdom of God; he is wrong in overlooking the fact...that the demonic powers can penetrate into the church itself, both in its doctrine and institutions. He is right to the extent in which he emphasizes the demonic element in every political structure of power..."

Theology of Peace
Paul Tillich
Edited and Introduced by Ronald H. Stone
Copies write 1990 Westminster/John Knox Press

An enormous loving thanks to my family and especially my girls who were born into this mess called pastoral ministry, not of their own free will or choice. They have not only survived as preacher's kids but have thrived. Meagan and Mikala are both amazing, wonderful Christians making their impact for God's Kingdom in this world.

I also thank God for getting us all through the various spiritual battles of my life. It was three years of abusive torture where my family felt like we were all in hand-to-hand combat with Satan himself/herself.

There is a lot of demonic bad behavior in the world today. We can find it at school, work, and sports and in the church where there are no consequences for toxic people because they hide behind grace but continue in their destructive conduct. This phenomenon reminds me of what is said in James 3:13-18:

"Who is wise and understanding among you? Let them show it by their good life, by deeds done in the humility that comes from wisdom. But if you harbor bitter envy and selfish ambition in your hearts, do not boast about it or deny the truth. Such 'wisdom' does not come down from heaven but is earthly, unspiritual, demonic. For where you have envy and selfish ambition, there you find disorder and every evil practice.

But the wisdom that comes from heaven is, first of all, pure; then peace-loving, considerate, submissive, full of mercy and good fruit, impartial and sincere. Peacemakers who sow in peace reap a harvest of righteousness." (NIV)

To all my clergy colleagues in ministry, keep up the good fight and do not let the venomous folks grind you down. We must remember that we are not fighting against flesh and blood. There is a force behind the negativity, and our focus must remain on Jesus, the author, and finisher of our faith. Remember when we are up to our buttocks in alligators, we were called to drain the pond. Yes, we are all called to word, sacrament, and order, but we are also called to fight to keep our churches from turning into the "Whore of Babylon" described in the Book of Revelation. My prayer is that this book will help us collectively, both laity and clergy, find wisdom and peace to enact the change that is needed for healthy relationships.

Enjoy the book!

Mike

INTRODUCTION

"For our struggle is not against flesh and blood, but against the rulers, against the powers, against the world forces of this darkness, against the spiritual forces of wickedness in the heavenly places". –The Apostle Paul (Ephesians 6:12 NIV)

"Evil is not to be traced back to the individual but to the collective behavior of humanity." --Reinhold Niebuhr

Do you know you are in a spiritual battle with evil every day? Do you know that the battles that wage around us are not only a part of our individual lives but also our corporate lives in the body of Christ? These battles are a part of our journey, our destiny and our calling in doing God's work. Let me just say, you can deny your purpose and the war that rages around you, but that does not mean that it is not happening. To acknowledge that spiritual warfare is around us and to engage in that war is a part of our Christian walk, life, testimony, inheritance and narrative. This war is fought on different fronts, with fluctuating degrees, and forces. We may not win all the battles, but we know, by the grace of God, we will win the war.

All battles are woven into the tapestry of our lives that eventually make up the big picture that God desires for us but that we, many times, cannot see in the here and the now. It is like a child looking through a knothole in a fence at the circus parade going through town. He sees the acrobats, and their crazy routines in the parade that make him laugh. He sees the bearded women and is amazed. He sees the lions and he is all of a sudden afraid. He sees an elephant, and he is astonished at its size. Then he is totally freaked out by the clowns with their painted faces. If we were to sit up in the tree by the fence, we could see the beginning, the middle, and the end of the parade. The spiritual world we live in is like that boy looking at that parade from the knothole. Life is all about perspective. Only God can see the big picture, but it is our responsibility to be aware of what is around us and trust that God has the best plans for our life.

We must believe that God knows the desires of our hearts including the desires that we do not even know. That is why it is imperative that we not only know that we are in a spiritual war but we need to be willing to fight. We need to develop some tactics to maneuver in this world to be battle ready. The spiritual world is real. The battle is being fought. The question is, do you want to engage in the warfare or live a life in denial of the war waging around you? To engage is the difference between being a victim of our circumstances or living victorious lives.

Jesus told us in Matthew 28:18 that, "All authority has been given to me in heaven and on earth." (NLT) As believers who trust in God, we have this confidence that we are free for joyful service to the Lord because the war has been won. We have victory in Jesus and grace saves us through faith in Jesus as God's Son. So my prayer is that this book will empower you to choose not to be a victim but to be victorious because the battle is ours!

1

LIVING IN THE HERE AND THE NOW

"In this life, we have to make many choices. Some are crucial, and some are not. Many of our choices are between good and evil. The choices we make, however, determine to a large extent our happiness or our unhappiness, because we have to live with the consequences of our choices." --James E. Faust

How we choose to live our lives is important. We can take the easy road and live in denial of the spiritual world around us and pretend it does not exist. The other day, I was at IHOP eating some of my favorite pancakes. The delicious harvest and grain pancakes make my stomach happy! To my right and across from me, there was this cute little girl sitting at a table and, for some reason, she was enamored with me. I guess I just look goofy or something. I remembered one of my daughters' favorite games to play when they were little was "Peek A Boo!" So, I took a napkin and unfolded it and held it before my face. Now to the toddler, I mysteriously disappeared and when I pulled it down and said "Peek A Boo", I suddenly re-appeared. For a child's mindset, this appeared to be magic. Every time I disappeared she was quiet and when I re-appeared she squealed with joy. I couldn't help but be reminded of Paul's analogy in 1 Corinthians 13:11, where he says "When I was a child, I spoke as a child, I understood as a child,

I thought as a child; but when I became a man, I put away childish things." (NKJV) We are at a time where we must all grow up and cease to play "Peek A Boo" with the spiritual world that surrounds us. We may try to mysteriously make spiritual warfare disappear, but it is there all the same. Here are some scriptures that unpack what this spiritual world looks like. So let us fold up the napkin and face the reality of the spiritual world in which we live.

I would like to have you read the following scriptures and then answer some questions about what these scriptures are teaching us. Read the following and let us discover the truth that God's wisdom reveals.

- Nehemiah 9:6: "You alone are the LORD. You made the skies and the heavens and all the stars. You made the earth and the seas and everything in them. You preserve them all, and the angels of heaven worship you." (NLT)
- Luke 2:13-15: "And suddenly there was with the angel a multitude of the heavenly host praising God and saying, "Glory to God in the highest, and on earth peace among those with whom he is pleased!" When the angels went away from them into heaven, the shepherds said to one another, "Let us go over to Bethlehem and see this thing that has happened, which the Lord has made known to us." (ESV)
- Ephesians 6:12: "For our struggle is not against flesh and blood, but against the rulers, against the authorities, against the powers of this dark world and the spiritual forces of evil in the heavenly realms." (NIV)
- Colossians 1:15-16: "Christ is the visible image of the invisible God. He had existed before anything was created and is supreme over all creation, for through him God created

everything in the heavenly realms and on earth. He made the things we can see and the things we can't see— such as thrones, kingdoms, rulers, and authorities in the unseen world. Everything was created through him and for him." (NLT)

- Hebrews 11:3: "By faith we understand that the universe was created by the word of God, so that what is seen was not made out of things that are visible." (ESV)

What do we specifically learn about angels from these scriptures?

Who is it that is besieging us?

Who are we combating?

How does Paul describe the "invisible world"?

Who gives us the perfect image of the invisible God?

Now, let's take a bigger look at what it is in which we Christians believe. We have been given an excellent synopsis in the historic confession of the Christian faith, the Apostle's Creed.

I believe in God, the Father almighty,
Creator of heaven and earth.

I believe in Jesus Christ, God's only Son, our Lord,
who was conceived by the Holy Spirit,
born of the Virgin Mary,
suffered under Pontius Pilate,

> *was crucified, died, and was buried;*
> *he descended into hell.*
> *On the third day, he rose again;*
> *he ascended into heaven,*
> *he is seated at the right hand of the Father,*
> *and he will come to judge the living and the dead.*

> *I believe in the Holy Spirit,*
> *the holy catholic Church,*
> *the communion of saints,*
> *the forgiveness of sins,*
> *the resurrection of the body,*
> *And the life everlasting. Amen.*

The very foundation of the Christian faith is to believe in Jesus Christ. Being the perfect, blemish-free sacrifice, Jesus is the Lamb of God and his death on the cross is the atonement for our sins. Because he was the fulfillment of our perfect prophet, priest, and King, you and I choose to make Him the Lord of our lives. He went to hell to break the chains of sin and death so that Satan would not have any more control over those areas, and to set the captives free. He was raised from the dead on the third day and conquered death so we can joyfully live forever with Jesus the Christ in heaven. This is for you! Not only was this gift of freedom for the times that Jesus lived in, it is a gift for ALL and His bell of freedom rings out into every century. There is no expiration date to His sacrifice. Satan no longer has control, however, we have become lost to that truth and the sound of that freedom is being silenced.

Paul's words found in I Corinthians 15:50-58 describe beautifully the benefits of the resurrection and also gives us a sense of urgency to stand firm and to work fervently for our Lord. Listen to these words carefully and consider them as truth for your soul:

"I declare to you, brothers and sisters, that flesh and blood cannot inherit the kingdom of God, nor does the perishable inherit the imperishable. Listen, I tell you a mystery: We will not all sleep, but we will all be changed—in a flash, in the twinkling of an eye, at the last trumpet. For the trumpet will sound, the dead will be raised imperishable, and we will be changed. For the perishable must clothe itself with the imperishable, and the mortal with immortality. When the perishable has been clothed with the imperishable, and the mortal with immortality, then the saying that is written will come true: "Death has been swallowed up in victory.

Where, O death, is your victory?

Where, O death, is your sting?"

The sting of death is sin, and the power of sin is the law. But thanks be to God! He gives us the victory through our Lord Jesus Christ. Therefore, my dear brothers and sisters, stand firm. Let nothing move you. Always give yourselves fully to the work of the Lord, because you know that your labor in the Lord is not in vain." (NIV)

What precisely is this spiritual realm that we cannot see but know is there? What is this Kingdom that we lose sight of because we are too busy focusing on the earthly realm? Let's look together at some Biblical examples. These pictures give us a glimpse into the spiritual realm that is very much a reality. Reflect on these passages with a theological eye and notice what is taking place in each situation.

- 2 Kings 6:11-17: The king of Aram became very upset over this. He called his officers together and demanded, "Which of you is the traitor? Who has been informing the king of

Israel of my plans?" "It's not us, my lord the king," one of the officers replied. "Elisha, the prophet in Israel, tells the king of Israel even the words you speak in the privacy of your bedroom!" "Go and find out where he is," the king commanded, "so I can send troops to seize him." And the report came back: "Elisha is at Dothan." So one night the king of Aram sent a great army with many chariots and horses to surround the city. When the servant of the man of God got up early the next morning and went outside, there were troops, horses, and chariots everywhere. "Oh, sir, what will we do now?" the young man cried to Elisha. "Don't be afraid!" Elisha told him. "For there are more on our side than on theirs!" Then Elisha prayed, "O LORD, open his eyes and let him see!" The LORD opened the young man's eyes, and when he looked up, he saw that the hillside around Elisha was filled with horses and chariots of fire. (NLT)

- My favorite comes from Daniel 10:7-17

"Only I, Daniel, saw this vision. The men with me saw nothing, but they were suddenly terrified and ran away to hide. So I was left there all alone to see this amazing vision. My strength left me, my face grew deathly pale, and I felt very weak. Then I heard the man speak, and when I heard the sound of his voice, I fainted and lay there with my face to the ground.

Just then a hand touched me and lifted me, still trembling, to my hands and knees. And the man said to me, "Daniel, you are very precious to God, so listen carefully to what I have to say to you. Stand up, for I have been sent to you." When he said this to me, I stood up, still trembling.

Then he said, "Don't be afraid, Daniel. Since the first day you began to pray for understanding and to humble yourself before your God, your request has been heard in heaven. I have come in answer to your prayer. But for twenty-one days the spirit prince of the kingdom of Persia blocked my way. Then Michael, one of the archangels, came to help me, and I left him there with the spirit prince of the kingdom of Persia. Now I am here to explain what will happen to your people in the future, for this vision concerns a time yet to come."

While he was speaking to me, I looked down at the ground, unable to say a word. Then the one who looked like a man touched my lips, and I opened my mouth and began to speak. I said to the one standing in front of me, "I am filled with anguish because of the vision I have seen, my lord, and I am very weak. How can someone like me, your servant, talk to you, my lord? My strength is gone, and I can hardly breathe." (NLT)

Wow! How long has it been since you have read a good story like that? Let's take a moment to talk about my namesake, the Archangel, Michael. In the Bible, only Michael, Gabriel, and Lucifer are named as angels and Michael is the only one called an archangel. Scripture tells us that Michael is "one of the chief princes," "the great prince," "a mighty warrior," and "leader of other angels." He is God's enforcer of law and judgment.

The meaning of the name Michael is a declarative question: "Who is like God?" His name is the opposite of the pride that caused Satan's fall. Isaiah 14: 12-15 tells the story and quotes Satan as saying: "I will ascend above the tops of the clouds; I will make myself like the Most High." (NIV) We see Satan in the garden tempting Adam and Eve again with pride in Gen 3:5b: "Your eyes will be opened, and you will be like God, knowing good and evil" (NIV) Michael points to the Lord – "Who is like God?" Satan points to himself saying: "I will be like God."

Michael appears to have a special role in safeguarding the nation of Israel and the Jewish people. In Jewish tradition, Michael is the author of Psalm 85, which is a sad poem about the suffering of the nation of Israel. He has also been connected with the "man" who spoke to Joshua at the battle of Jericho.[1] In his role as chief warrior angel, I believe it will be Michael's voice that will announce the return of Jesus to earth. Church tradition states that it was Michael who fought with and threw Satan out of Heaven when Satan revolted against God and tried to take God's place. After this defeat, Michael then became the "top angel" and took over Satan's place.

The stories above represent two different scenarios of activity that are taking place in the invisible realm around us. God allowed these men to bridge the gap in the physical realm to see into the spiritual realm.[2] The Lord released the eyes of Elisha's servant to understand the host of God's army. Elisha's spiritual eyes were able to see that there was spiritual warfare taking place all around him. Daniel saw the angel standing before him, and everyone else was scared to death and ran out of the palace. Daniel was allowed by God to see and receive the prophecy from the angel about the future.

The good news about these Scriptures is that God is with us in the midst of this unseen spiritual realm and that God's good angels are here to help us to fight against the evil demonic angels of Satan. We must realize that demonic angels are what we are fighting, not necessarily what we can see. Collective evil can manipulate people to try to harm us and, if we realize the source, we can be battle ready against that demonic force that is ravaging us! The spiritual realm affects the physical realm, so when things go amok, that should be a red light on the dashboard of our lives to pay attention and get engaged in spiritual warfare.

What I am about to tell you is huge! The Bible explicitly warns against the practice of being spiritually attracted to things that are not holy and of God. Demonic angels are given rights to oppress and possess people based upon your participation in occult practices. The demonic, angelic forces want to deceive people into believing that they can have supernatural power over people (past and present) and can use divination to know the future. Witchcraft, horoscopes, Ouija boards, tarot cards and psychic phenomenon can seem innocent on the surface yet are an extremely dangerous influence causing great harm to those who get involved. When you get involved with these venues of demonic oppression, you are giving Satan the right to enter into your life, your home, your work and your family. You must stay away. These are not Hollywood fantasies, they are real, and this is not a game! To participate in these activities is something that the Bible clearly warns us not to do. Do not be involve in these things because to do so is to deny that God has your best interest at heart and that God has no control of the future. It is to deny God's power for a false power that has been judged and condemned. I want to back up what I am saying with what scripture says, so for those of you who believe that fortune telling, horoscopes and Ouija boards are harmless fun, let's look at what the Bible has to say.

- Leviticus 19:26: "Do not eat any meat with the blood still in it." "Do not practice divination or sorcery." (NIV)
- Leviticus 19:31: "Do not turn to mediums or seek out spiritualists, for you will be defiled by them. I am the LORD your God." (NIV)

- Deuteronomy 18:9-14: "When you enter the land the LORD your God is giving you, be very careful not to imitate the detestable customs of the nations living there. For example, never sacrifice your son or daughter as a burnt offering. And do not let your people practice fortune-telling, or use sorcery, or interpret omens, or engage in witchcraft, or cast spells, or function as mediums or psychics, or call forth the spirits of the dead. Anyone who does these things is detestable to the LORD. It is because the other nations have done these detestable things that the LORD your God will drive them out ahead of you. But you must be blameless before the LORD your God. The nations you are about to displace consult sorcerers and fortune-tellers, but the LORD your God forbids you to do such things." (NLT)

- Deuteronomy 18: 11-12 "Let no one be found among you who sacrifices his son or daughter in the fire, who practices divination or sorcery, interprets omens, engages in witchcraft, or casts spells, or who is a medium or spiritist or who consults the dead. Anyone who does these things is detestable to the LORD, and because of these detestable practices the LORD your God will drive out those nations before you." (NIV)

- 1 Chronicles 10:13-14 "Saul died because he was unfaithful to the LORD; he did not keep the word of the LORD and even consulted a medium for guidance, and did not inquire of the LORD. So the LORD put him to death and turned the kingdom over to David son of Jesse."

Folks, I am here to tell you that these invisible or unseen forces are real. Good and evil is all around us vying for our attention, leading us into destruction, or victorious, joyful living. If we believe in

Jesus Christ, then we believe that He died to subjugate the demonic shenanigans of the devil, and Jesus' blood atonement has truly set us free from the evil demonic forces that desire to bind us. Jesus did not have to come and die on a cross to save us if we did not need saving, protecting, and guidance. There are forces, both angelic and demonic, that are actively working around us. Jesus told us to pray for God's will to be done on earth as it is in heaven. We even ask as Jesus taught us to pray that He would "deliver us from evil." Jesus told Simon Peter that the gates of hell will not prevail against the work that God has purposed for us to accomplish, as God's will is being worked out in our lives.

- In Matthew 16:13-20, when Jesus came to the region of Caesarea Philippi, he asked his disciples, "Who do people say the Son of Man is?"
- They replied, "Some say John the Baptist; others say Elijah; and still others, Jeremiah or one of the prophets."
- "But what about you?" he asked. "Who do you say I am?"
- Simon Peter answered, "You are the Messiah, the Son of the living God."
- Jesus replied, "Blessed are you, Simon son of Jonah, for this was not revealed to you by flesh and blood, but by my Father in heaven. And I tell you that you are Peter, and on this rock I will build my church, and the gates of Hades will not overcome it. I will give you the keys of the kingdom of heaven; whatever you bind on earth will be bound in heaven, and whatever you loose on earth will be loosed in heaven." Then he ordered his disciples not to tell anyone that he was the Messiah. (NIV)

Today I ask you, who do you say Jesus is?

Will you accept the keys that God has given you through the sacrifice of His only Son, Jesus?

Do you bind things in your prayer life and engage in spiritual warfare?

When Jesus says: "The gates of hell will not overcome the church," what does that look like to you?

Even though Scripture says that the gates of hell will not prevail. We are still called to rattle the gates of hell for souls for Jesus, and when we do this, we all will face opposition. It is not a matter of if but when. We need to understand that the battle is not against flesh and blood but powers in the heavenly places. As we begin to receive a divine awakening like Daniel of the spiritual warfare around us, may God grant us the ability to understand how the enemy moves against us in the physical, earthly realm.

If you have accepted Christ as your savior, you are a target. The evil one does not want you to succeed and wants to thwart your efforts in bringing about the Kingdom of God on earth. Evil wants to keep you from exposing the corruption that is going on in the kingdom of this world. You are now engaged in a conflict between the two kingdoms. Maybe the following illustration will better explain what I mean.

If I went duck hunting with my black lab and I hit some ducks and they were down on the ground I would be very happy knowing my dog was fetching them. However, if there were still a flock in the air around me, I would continue to shoot at some more ducks instead of going after the ones on the ground because I know the ones on the ground I already have but the ones in the air are getting away. I believe the devil works in the same way. He knows non-Christians are already on the ground, and are not a threat. All he needs is his demonic minions to deliver them to him. However, we Christians are getting away. Therefore, we are a viable and active moving target and can expect a demonic assault. We are the moving targets that would be grand prizes if evil were to take us out. The good news is, he cannot capture us. He has already lost that war and he is the one that is frustrated. I love how Wesley said it in his sermon on Evil Angels. Wesley explains that we are forever a threat to Satan and as that target, he works to destroy us twenty-four hours a day, seven days a week and does not give up. However, we have a mighty God that works even harder to cover us and protect us. "A constant watch he keeps; he eyes them night and day; he never slumbers, never sleeps, lest he should lose his prey." [3]

I am going to be very real with you and let you know that I do not like talking about spiritual warfare at all. Every time I talk about being battle ready for spiritual warfare it makes the Devil mad, and weird things happen so l want you to know I have been praying for safety and protection for those who read this book and for me as I teach it and share it with others. But I also know that I serve a mighty God who has put a hedge of protection around me and we cannot be shaken. Psalm 136:12 states "with a strong hand and an outstretched arm, for his steadfast love endures forever;" (ESV)

We are faced today with the influx of people from other places in the world that believe in many different gods and I believe this has invited more demonic activity into our society than we have ever seen before or imagined. All of these gods, in my opinion, are demonic manifestations designed to guide people away from the truth of Christ. Paul tells Timothy in 1 Timothy 4:1 "Now the Holy Spirit tells us clearly that in the last times some will turn away from what we believe; they will follow lying spirits and teachings that comes from demons."(NLT) We have people today that are reviving and practicing many of the ancient occult rituals from all around the world. With all this going on in our multi-cultural world, we are letting a lot of bad-behaving demons have free reign as we throw Jesus out the door to be politically correct and accepting of all religions as being another way to God. In John 14:6, Jesus answered, "I am the way and the truth and the life. No one comes to the Father except through me." (NIV) Jesus was definitive when he said this. "I am the way" means that no other person has direct access to God but through Jesus and when we come to God through the access we have in Jesus Christ and his sacrifice, we will have instant connection to truth and life. You only need watch the news for thirty minutes these days to render a reality that the world needs more truth and more life. On the Day of Pentecost, the Apostle Peter proclaimed about Jesus: Acts 4.12 "Salvation is found in no one else, for there is no other name under heaven given to men by which we must be saved." (NIV) That is why Paul affirms this fact to his protégé': 1 Timothy 2.5-6 "For there is one God and one mediator between God and mankind, the man Christ Jesus, who gave himself as a ransom for all people." (NIV)

Please do not misunderstand me, I love living in a multicultural society and enjoy the unique experiences that multicultural living brings. I strive toward and promote multicultural peace among all people because we are all created in the image of God. Developing cross-cultural relationships and fostering understanding is not only important, it is a great experience to learn about other cultures, beliefs, traditions, art, literature, and history. But there is a difference between culture and the spiritual realm. Within each culture is a heart waiting to connect with their creator. And Jesus says "I am that way." Blending cultures does not mean we blend the spiritual realm. With all that said, I hold true to the Divine revelation given to me through Jesus Christ, and that is that the only real peace that can take place in our lives and communities comes through faith in Jesus as God's Son and our Savior. In no way does this diminish my friendships with people from other cultures but I do have a God-given desire for self-preservation, and I want to protect myself from harmful radicals that wish to destroy me for my belief in Jesus Christ.

When I was growing up, we heard about demonic activity from our Missionaries in Africa battling witch doctors and having to face the demons surrounding a temple in India where they were sacrificing food and small animals to a monkey god. After being in ministry twenty-seven years, I can see that demonic activity is more prevalent and becoming more mainstream in America's culture.

Spiritual warfare is not like Hollywood portrays! I have had personal situations where I have seen demonic activity pass through the front of my home. It was like a super dark figure that was darker than the darkness of the room. It floated from the formal living room through a wall and down the hallway. Mikala, my college-age daughter, and I have both experienced that dark figure in our bedrooms at night hovering up in the corner and awakening us from a deep sleep. We both prayed and rebuked the evil spirits in Jesus' name, and they have immediately gone away. We both have prayed to God to let him know that we do not like to see the spiritual warfare that is raging around us. This visible demonic activity is not normal but has happened when we have been experiencing a lot of problems in the physical world usually dealing with toxic people that were being psychologically abusive by bullying, gossiping, and mobbing us. It always seemed that the problems we saw happening to us in the physical realm were also happening in the spiritual realm. So, in my opinion, they are connected.

I do not understand why one young teenager who participated in some Ouija board activities can become chock full of demons and demonic oppression, and another kid who did the same had no demonic activity in his/her life at all. The same with people that participate in devil worship or participated in revived ancient pagan occults. Some are deep into it and cut themselves and bleed on altars, break into churches and desecrate a church altar, sacrifice cats, and nothing ever happens. They want satanic power and it is never given to them yet another person that participates just once manifests demonic activity and false power over some non-Christian individuals.

I do know, that if you have ever been involved or participated in these types of activities, you need to rebuke those past events in Jesus' name. Then ask God to forgive you for trying to seek wisdom, power, and happiness from other places other than the one true source of wisdom, power, hope, and joy that comes from God the Father, God the Son, and God the Holy Spirit. You do not want any demonic strongholds in your life. When you do this, it is just like we used to train dogs in the old days not to poop or pee in the house. When we confess our sin to Jesus and rebuke past bad occult behavior, it is like taking Satan and sticking his nose in his poop in your life, and he/she goes away because now you are forgiven and Satan, and his poop, are gone and no longer have a foothold in your life. If you do not ask for forgiveness and rebuke this behavior in Jesus' name, then it gives Satan a handle on your heart, and he can easily grab that handle and throw you onto the ground into the poop very easily. This story is good for all sin battles that we experience in our lives! Keep asking for forgiveness and keep rebuking in Jesus' name because we have victory in Jesus.

I want to invite you, right now at this very moment, to take time now and confess your participation if you did. Know that "no man condemns you"... (John 8:10-11 NIV). You have been bought with a price and God has so much more planned for you.

Now, rebuke the occasion in Jesus' name.

Pray for forgiveness and for the Holy Spirit to fill your life and give you wisdom and strength.

> Satan, I rebuke you in Jesus' name, and I am closing any doors, which my ancestors or I may have opened to you and your demons. I renounce Satan and all his demons; I declare them to be my enemies, and I want them out of my life completely.
>
> In the name of Jesus Christ, I now claim deliverance from any and all evil spirits, which may be in me. Once and for all I close the door in my life to all occult practices and command all connected and related spirits to leave me now, never to return in the name of Jesus. Amen.[4]

2

THE STRUGGLE IS REAL

"Our life always expresses the result of our dominant thought." --Soren Kierkegaard

A common saying today among our youth is "It's about to get real up in here!" In fact, Toyota has based an entire commercial on this catch phrase. Our struggle is real and this struggle is made evident in the Bible. When we see the phrase *"the world"* in the Bible, it is talking about people who live on planet earth. Those of us that live on planet earth have real struggles! Paul knew this, he lived it out the multiple times he was chastised, imprisoned and rejected. So when Paul tells us not to conform to the patterns of this world (Romans 12:2), he is referring to how the people collectively choose to live on the earth. We, as believers, are told not to conform to the patterns of how others live but to exist to please God, who is not of this world. Jesus is saying a prayer for all of us as he makes his way to Jerusalem and his death on a cross: "I have given them Your word; and the world has hated them because they are not of the world, just as I am not of the world. I do not pray that You should take them out of the world, but that You should keep them from the evil one. They are not of the world, just as I am not of the world." (John 17:14-16 NIV) We are called "to live in the world but not be a part of the world." In this passage, we see the two kingdoms in conflict: The Kingdom of God and the kingdom of this world. There is wickedness in this world, and it comes from "the patterns" of this world. Theologian Reinhold Niebuhr said it best: "Evil is not to be traced back to the individual but to the collective behavior of humanity."

We see in this prayer Jesus prays for us, that spiritual warfare is serious business. John 17: 6-26:

- "I have manifested Your name to the men whom You have given Me out of the world. They were Yours, You gave them to Me, and they have kept Your word. Now they have known that all things which You have given Me are from You. For I have given to them the words which You have given Me; and they have received them, and have known surely that I came forth from You; and they have believed that You sent

Me. "I pray for them. I do not pray for the world but for those whom You have given Me, for they are Yours. And all Mine are Yours, and Yours are Mine, and I am glorified in them. Now I am no longer in the world, but these are in the world, and I come to You. Holy Father, keep through Your name those whom You have given Me, that they may be one as We are. While I was with them in the world, I kept them in Your name. Those whom You gave Me I have kept; and none of them is lost except the son of perdition, that the Scripture might be fulfilled. But now I come to You, and these things I speak in the world, that they may have My joy fulfilled in themselves. I have given them Your word; and the world has hated them because they are not of the world, just as I am not of the world. I do not pray that You should take them out of the world, but that You should keep them from the evil one. They are not of the world, just as I am not of the world. Sanctify them by Your truth. Your word is truth. As You sent Me into the world, I also have sent them into the world. And for their sakes I sanctify Myself, that they also may be sanctified by the truth. "I do not pray for these alone, but also for those who will believe in Me through their word; that they all may be one, as You, Father, are in Me, and I in You; that they also may be one in Us, that the world may believe that You sent Me. And the glory which You gave Me I have given them, that they may be one just as We are one: I in them, and You in Me; that they may be made perfect in one, and that the world may know that You have sent Me, and have loved them as You have loved Me. "Father, I desire that they also whom You gave Me may be with Me where I am, that they may behold My glory which

You have given Me; for You loved Me before the foundation of the world. O righteous Father! The world has not known You, but I have known You; and these have known that You sent Me. And I have declared to them Your name, and will declare it, that the love with which You loved Me may be in them, and I in them." (NKJV)

According to what Jesus lays out in this scripture, what is our job in this world?

How are we to relate to the world?

What does Jesus request for our benefit and support?

Jesus has our best interest at heart. Go back and circle Jesus' encouraging words.

I do not know about you, but after reading John 17, it becomes apparent that if we are in the world but not of this world, we are going to have conflicts. Those conflicts are spiritual warfare. Our problem is not God's created nature that surrounds us; rather it is the spiritual forces of light and darkness that affect us in the conflicting battle for control. As children of God, we are stuck in this tension between these two kingdoms in conflict. Since we belong to God through Jesus Christ, then we are in the midst of the battle. The prayer of John 17 expresses the heart of Jesus. Jesus knows the battles that are going to ravage our souls. Jesus also understands that the world despises him and that the world will also despise anyone who follows him. Come what may, we are sent into the world to be a witness and to share the "Good News" of our Savior. To not to be of this world is to be counter-cultural. We do not avoid the culture but live in it to influence others to have a relationship with the Divine through Jesus Christ. This is something we have to do as Christians. Victory is ours through Jesus and the guidance of the indwelling of the Holy Spirit in our lives. We have to work collectively within the body of Christ to discern what is right and what is wrong. We live in a black and white world, not a world of gray!

- "Beloved, do not believe every spirit, but test the spirits to see whether they are from God, for many false prophets have gone out into the world. By this, you know the Spirit of God: every spirit that confesses that Jesus Christ has come in the flesh is from God, and every spirit that does not confess Jesus is not from God. This is the spirit of the antichrist, which you heard was coming and now is in the world already. Little children, you are from God and have overcome them, for he who is in you is greater than he who is in the world. They are from the world; therefore they speak from the world, and the world listens to them." (1 John 4:1-21 ESV)

We have to be transformed by the renewing of our mind to understand God's ways.

- Rom. 12:2: "Do not conform to the pattern of this world, but be transformed by the renewing of your mind. Then you will be able to test and approve what God's will is—his good, pleasing and perfect will." (NIV)

We are not to live according to the patterns of this present evil age. Rather we should follow Paul's command to keep on being transformed by the renewing of our minds. This is a total change from the inside out. Matter of fact, the Greek verb "transformed" (μεταμορφοῦσθε) is translated into English as "metamorphosis." The most crucial part of this metamorphosis is our "mind". In the Greek culture of the day, that meant that we needed to change our attitudes, our thoughts, our feelings, and our actions. The way we keep our minds constantly being made new is by being involved in Christian fellowship and discipleship by inputting into our mind prayer, Bible study, worship, holy communion, and giving to God's work of our time, talent, gifts, and service. This Christian lifestyle keeps us transforming into Jesus' likeness.

When we live in this state of transformation, then we will be able to prove by testing what God's will is—His good, pleasing and perfect will. God's will is what is good! Only by being metamorphosed spiritually can a Christian ascertain, do, and enjoy the will of God. Jesus knew that Satan would use every kind of enticement possible to lure our hearts away from God. Jesus also knew how difficult it would be for those who believe in Him to remain faithful due to the concerns of the world.[5] The battles of spiritual warfare are intense when a person decides to accept Jesus as their Savior. The enemy will attack from all sides, hoping to dissuade the person from fully giving their heart to Jesus. The enemy will use circumstances, events, people, things and even doubt in our minds to steal our heart back to his ways. Once we are made aware of the world's influences and how they are in opposition to God's ways, we must then learn how to operate in the world as a true follower of Christ.

Let's look at James 4:1-4:

- "What is causing the quarrels and fights among you? Don't they come from the evil desires at war within you? You want what you don't have, so you scheme and kill to get it. You are jealous of what others have, but you can't get it, so you fight and wage war to take it away from them. Yet you don't have what you want because you don't ask God for it. And even when you ask, you don't get it because your motives are all wrong—you want only what will give you pleasure. You adulterers! Don't you realize that friendship with the world makes you an enemy of God? I say it again: If you want to be a friend of the world, you make yourself an enemy of God." (NLT)

How do we become an enemy of God?

How can we apply the metamorphosis of the renewing of our mind to conquer the desires of the world?

Pray the following:

Almighty God, the Father of mercies and God of all comfort, come to my help and deliver me from this difficulty that assails me. I believe, Lord, that all trials of life are under your care and that all things work for the good of those who love You. Take away from me fear, anxiety and distress. Help me to face and endure my difficulty with faith, courage and wisdom. Grant that this trial may bring me closer to You for You are my rock and refuge, my comfort and hope, my delight and joy. I trust in Your love and compassion. Blessed is Your name, Father, Son and Holy Spirit, now and forever. Amen.[6]

3

THE KINGDOM OF GOD IS AT HAND

"For we do continually beseech God by Jesus Christ to preserve us from the demons which are hostile to the worship of God, and whom we of old time served, in order that, after our conversion by Him to God, we may be blameless. For we call Him Helper and Redeemer, the power of whose name even the demons do fear; and at this day, when they are exorcised in the name of Jesus Christ, crucified under Pontius Pilate, governor of Judea, they are overcome. And thus it is manifest to all, that His Father has given Him so great power, by virtue of which demons are subdued to His name, and to the dispensation of His suffering." --St. Justin Martyr (Dialogue With Trypho, 30).

I love the gospel of Mark. It gets straight to the point. Mark reminds me of a show I watched growing up, "Dragnet", and today you can still watch it on "Nick at Night." Dragnet is a show about the ins and outs of police detective work. A famous line from the main character, Sergeant Joe Friday, is "Just the facts, ma'am." He is telling people: "Spare me the details and the drama and just tell me what happened." Mark writes his gospel in the same manner: "Just the facts, just Jesus' actions, I just want to hear from the eyewitnesses. Spare me the details and boil it down and give it to me straight."

Mark, needless to say, is not a detailed person like Luke where we find a tremendous amount of details and loads of background material that is left out of the book of Mark. For example, Mark skips the birth narrative altogether and goes straight to Jesus being baptized by John the Baptist. Mark only mentions four of Jesus' forty-six parables and eighteen miracles out of thirty-six. If Mark gives us any details, then they are paramount. I find it interesting, for Mark, the major details in his Gospel that make known that the Kingdom of God is at hand are Jesus' actions of being an authoritative teacher, his healing power over diseases and disabilities, his authority over demons by casting them out, his ability to control demons by telling them what to do, and his ability to conquer death. The Kingdom of God is at hand because Jesus has power over the kingdoms of this world and that proves that Jesus is the Son of God. Let's look at one of Mark's major proofs that Jesus is God's Son: His ability to have power and authority over Satan and his demons.

Read Mark 1:12-13. Right after Jesus' baptism, the Holy Spirit sends him out into the desert to be tempted by Satan. He is out there for forty days. A number that is reflective of Moses and Israel wandering in the wilderness for forty years, Moses also spent forty days on Mt. Sinai receiving the Ten Commandments from God. It is all a revealing time for Jesus of the tactics that the enemy is using against him. This is the start of the many demonic battles Jesus faces throughout the Gospel of Mark. The good news is each and every time Jesus conquers and does not fall prey to Satan. Jesus was one hundred percent God and one hundred percent human at the same time.

What human-like characteristics did Jesus have to which you can relate?

How have you experienced your adversary, Satan, trying to trip you up?

Read Mark 1:39. Jesus' mission, according to Mark, was to preach (he often did this in the local synagogues), and to cast out demons. How did this give authority and authenticity of his Divinity?

How does Mark show the Kingdom of God *embreaking*[7] into the world?

Read Mark 1:21-28. After Jesus calls four of his disciples to follow him, he plunged headlong into his first ministry experience, and that was to cast out an evil spirit from the man in the synagogue.

The act of casting out the demon demonstrated what two characteristics about Jesus teaching?

What did he tell the evil spirit to do?

Why do you think it is important that Jesus ordered the evil spirit to be quiet?

Read Mark 3:10-12.
What did the evil spirits do when they encountered Jesus?

What did Jesus order the evil spirits to do? Why?

Read Mark 3:13-19. I find it very comforting that Jesus often went up on a mountain to teach the disciples or give them some divine revelation. I, too, find mountains to be peaceful and to be a great place to be reflective and to talk and listen to God. This scene is crucial because Jesus calls them to be with him so he could disciple them, to be sent out to preach, and to have Divine authority to drive out demons.

What inspires you to seek out God and be reflective?

Jesus chose twelve to prepare for this new Kingdom of God. Why is this significant?

Why is "Authority" an important aspect for Jesus to have in Mark's gospel?

What future application does it have for believers today?

Now continue to read verses 20-30 of Mark 3. Once again we see the religious institution in the Gospel of Mark on the wrong side of history and acting as Satan's pawns. They accused the Son of God of being possessed by an evil spirit and working for Satan! Even Jesus' family thinks he is insane and tries to entrap him and take him back home. Satan is doing everything he can to stop Jesus, even using his family and religious leaders against him. Jesus defends himself by calling out the absurdity of the religious leaders' logic.

What logic does Jesus use to expose the lie and shed light on the truth about Satan and evil spirits?

What analogy does Jesus use?

Read Mark 5:1-20.

When you look at all of the details and drama in this story, what important concepts do you believe Mark is trying to emphasize?

How do you think the demon-possessed man felt meeting Jesus and being set free?

What did you learn about demons by reading the conversation between Jesus and the demons?

Who was going to torture the demons if they left?

Why were the people afraid?

Why did they ask Jesus to leave?

How many times does economic loss keep people from doing the right thing, or even worse, to shun Jesus and Christianity?

Read Mark 6:7–13.

Jesus sent the disciples in groups of two to help him in His Galilean ministry, and he gives them authority over what?

What did they do?

Read Mark 7: 24–30. Here we see Jesus head to Tyre for some seclusion, rest and to spend some one-on-one time with his disciples, teaching them and unpacking their experiences. He didn't want anyone to know he was there, but he couldn't keep his presence a secret. A Greek woman begs Jesus to get the demon out of her daughter. Jesus tells her he is here to take care of the disciples and not foreigners. He uses the example of a family having a meal together and how they do not need to be interrupted by the family pet dog for food. The woman was persistent and had great faith and humility.

What was her response to Jesus?

What happened to the little girl?

What do we learn from this demon exorcism?

Read Mark 8:31–33. Jesus' mission is to make his way to the cross. We find Satan once again tempting Jesus to take another route just like in the temptations he experienced in the wilderness.

What does Jesus tell Peter?

What is the contrast here between the things of God versus the things of men?

Read Mark 9:14-29. In these verses we see Jesus enter into the scene to find some of the disciples arguing with scribes who obviously were unbelieving and were starting arguments with the disciples. The people notice Jesus and run to him with excitement. A man tells Jesus that his disciples could not cast the demon out of his boy. Jesus does what the disciples could not. Later, in private, Jesus tells the disciples that their failure was a lack of depending on God's power through prayer.

Picture yourself as the parent in this story with your very own sick child. We would be claiming, "I do believe! Help my unbelief!" All things are possible with God!

When Jesus lifted the boy to his feet, do you see any foreshadowing in this story?

Some demons need what to be cast out?

Read Mark 9: 38-41. The disciples are very concerned that people other than them are casting out demons in Jesus' name.

What was Jesus' response?

How can we be more receiving of Christian believers who are not a part of our circle of friends?

How can we better learn that people who stand against evil are on our team?

Read Mark 16:9.

For the first time in the Gospel of Mark we are told that Jesus did what to Mary Magdalene?

Why does Mark tell us this fact here and not the three previous times he mentions Mary Magdalene?

What is the importance of Mary being the first to experience the Risen Christ?

Read Mark 16:17.

What are the five signs of believers?

1.

2.

3.

4.

5.

Believers are to do this in _____ _____!

WARNING: Back in Jesus' day, apparently there were those who persecuted Christians and others by forcing them to handle snakes and drink poison. This ability is a sign of Divine protection under duress, not something to do to prove that you are a Christian.

Pray this prayer from the "Rite of Exorcism" from the Roman Catholic Church (modernized by me).

I cast you out, unclean spirit, along with every Satanic power of the enemy, every evil spirit from hell, and all your fallen companions; in the name of our Lord Jesus Christ. Be gone and stay far from this creature of God. For it is God who commands you; God who flung you headlong from the heights of heaven into the depths of hell. It is God who commands you; God, who once stilled the sea and the wind and the storm. Listen to me, and tremble in fear, Satan, you enemy of the faith, you foe of the human race, you begetter of death, you robber of life, you corrupter of justice, you root of all evil and vice; seducer of men, betrayer of the nations, instigator of envy, font of avarice, instigator of discord, author of pain and sorrow. Why, then, do you stand and resist, knowing as you must that Christ the Lord brings your plans to nothing? Fear Him, who in Isaac was offered in sacrifice, in Joseph, sold into bondage, slain as the paschal lamb, crucified as man, yet triumphed over the powers of hell. *(The three signs of the cross, which follow, are traced on the brow of the possessed person.)* Begone then, in the name of the Father, and of the Son, and of the Holy Spirit. Give place to the Holy Spirit by this sign of the holy cross of our Lord Jesus Christ, who lives and reigns with the Father and the Holy Spirit, God, forever and ever.[8]

4

AUTHORITY OVER EVIL

"To learn strong faith is to endure great trials. I have learned my faith by standing firm amid severe testings." --George Mueller

Since we are supposed to be in the world but not of the world, we are not to live cloistered, closeted lives in hiding from the world but rather we are supposed to be a part of the world. However, as we are a part of this world, we are expected to be counter-cultural by living our lives after the example of Jesus. While we are in the world, we are supposed to be telling folks the good news of Jesus and to be battle ready. What we are dealing with are kingdoms in conflict, the kingdom of this world versus God's Kingdom. A great snapshot of what this looks like is in the Gospel of Luke. In one of the more mysterious verses of Luke, Jesus tells His disciples, "I saw Satan fall like lightning from heaven." (Luke 10:18 NLT). Let's look at the whole story and ascertain how we can make "Satan fall like lightning from heaven" as described in Luke 10:1-20:

- "The Lord now chose seventy-two other disciples and sent them ahead in pairs to all the towns and places he planned to visit. These were his instructions to them: "The harvest is great, but the workers are few. So pray to the Lord who is in charge of the harvest; ask him to send more workers into his fields. Now go, and remember that I am sending you out as lambs among wolves. Don't take any money with you, or a traveler's bag, or an extra pair of sandals. And don't stop to greet anyone on the road."

  "Whenever you enter someone's home, first say, 'May God's peace be on this house.' If those who live there are peaceful, the blessing will stand; if they are not, the blessing will return to you. Don't move around from home to home. Stay in one place, eating and drinking what they provide. Don't hesitate to accept hospitality, because those who work deserve their pay.

  "If you enter a town, and it welcomes you, eat whatever is set before you. Heal the sick, and tell them, 'The Kingdom of God is near you now.' But if a town refuses to welcome you, go out into its streets and say, 'We wipe even the dust of your town from our feet to show that we have abandoned you to your fate. And know this—the Kingdom of God is near!' I assure you, even wicked Sodom will be better off than such a town on judgment day.

"What sorrow awaits you, Korazin and Bethsaida! For if the miracles I did in you had been done in wicked Tyre and Sidon, their people would have repented of their sins long ago, clothing themselves in burlap and throwing ashes on their heads to show their remorse. Yes, Tyre and Sidon will be better off on judgment day than you. And you people of Capernaum, will you be honored in heaven? No, you will go down to the place of the dead."

Then he said to the disciples, "Anyone who accepts your message is also accepting me. And anyone who rejects you is rejecting me. And anyone who rejects me is rejecting God, who sent me."

When the seventy-two disciples returned, they joyfully reported to him, "Lord, even the demons obey us when we use your name!" "Yes," he told them, "I saw Satan fall from heaven like lightning! Look, I have given you authority over all the power of the enemy, and you can walk among snakes and scorpions and crush them. Nothing will injure you. But don't rejoice because evil spirits obey you; rejoice because your names are registered in heaven." (NLT)

When theologians look at this scripture, they see different possibilities concerning the time period Jesus was referring when he said: "I saw Satan fall from the sky like lightning". Was Jesus reflecting upon the time when Satan fell before Jesus came to earth and Michael and Satan had it out and Satan was thrown from Heaven as mentioned in Genesis? Was Jesus doing foreshadowing to the end of time when Satan will be thrown into the abyss, and we will no longer have to deal with evil again? Or was Jesus talking about the present time when he saw the disciples go out two by two to heal and preach and the disciples came back excited because they had command over the evil spirits? The great news is all three views reveal to us that Satan loses. He has already been judged and will be condemned.

I believe Jesus is talking about an instant viewing as the disciples were battling with the kingdom of the world and the power of the Kingdom of God was overcoming the evil in the world. There is no reference in the Old Testament of anyone casting out demons. It is a New Testament phenomenon showing that there is a connection between the two kingdoms and they are in conflict. We also see that God's Kingdom overcomes the worldly kingdom because Jesus and his disciples are given authority to cast out demons (evil spirits). In the book of Mark, as the "Kingdom of God" is proclaimed, the demons manifest themselves. Throughout the gospels, we see this battle between the two kingdoms that are in conflict. In Luke, Jesus is the "strong man" that can bind the demons and cast them into pigs. In the lightning scripture, it is evident that Jesus gave the disciples authority to continue to break forth the Kingdom of God over the kingdom of the world.

This brings us to a third option that is my personal view. That when Jesus saw "Satan fall like lightning" it was a present reality. Even today Satan's demons continue to demonstrate Jesus' power over darkness by allowing us to have authority over demons. This text is also a foreshadowing of the day when all this battle will finally be over, and evil will no longer be prevalent in our lives and world.

Now let us consider the practical theology here. Jesus intends us to go out two by two. There are no solo "Rambos" in this new

Kingdom of God. We are commissioned to "Go" forth to preach and heal and have dominion over demons. The disciples were so elated with the results of preaching "in Jesus' Name" that they came back to Jesus giddy. Jesus said: "Yea, I saw it too, I saw Satan fall from the sky like lightning because you were going out in ministering in my name and Satan's strongholds were falling from the sky just like it will continue until the day of final judgment and Satan's kingdom is no more." (Luke 10:1:18 paraphrased)

So it is important that when we preach (tell others how God has been made real in our lives), heal (pray for people to be healed), and cast out demons (rebuke Satan) that we do it all in Jesus' name.

We are God's Disciples, and we are called to be the light of God's Kingdom that shatters the darkness of the kingdom of this world. When we go out and do God's Kingdom work, we are waging war with evil and sometimes this work causes demons to manifest themselves. However, we need not fear because "'As surely as I live,' says the Lord, 'every knee will bow before me; every tongue will acknowledge God.'" (Romans 14:11 NIV)

One time I was preaching at a youth worship service. The Holy Spirit was moving in such a way it was palpable. About half way back in the sanctuary a demon manifested itself in a girl. She just slipped under a pew and was shouting: "She is mine, you cannot have her." Now let me just say you do not want to have a spectacle take place when this happens. Rather, a couple of youth counselors took her into a Sunday school room and calmed her down. I finished the service and, when all the kids had left, I went into the Sunday school room. Doing this kind of work is like "open heart surgery". It is nasty, and you want mature Christian people around who can pray. This girl had strongholds because she did not forgive her mom and her mom's boyfriends who had allowed her to be abused as a little girl. She tried to dull the pain in her life by filling it with all the wrong stuff. She also participated in some witchcraft rituals. So what you have to do is ask the demon what foothold they have in the life of the individual, and they will tell you. Then you ask the individual to renounce the sin in Jesus' name and to ask for forgiveness. The demon then does not have a foothold any longer and leaves. It usually gets messy because there is usually more than one foothold and we find out private things about the individual. So it has to be done with great care and love. The follow up is also intensive. You have to bring in the parents, line the individual up with Christian counseling and deal with the authorities concerning the abuse.

Like I said earlier, the more we have the occult practiced, and pagan religions proliferate in our culture, the more of this demonic possession activity we are going to see as people come and seek a relationship with Christ to free themselves from this horrible bondage.

There was another time when two young men came into my office and said that one of the men's girlfriend was demon possessed. They said they had been up all night with her praying and rebuking the evil spirit but that it would not leave. The evil spirit was trying to harm the young lady by making her damage her body by throwing her on the ground, cutting herself, and other bad behavior. She was also an ex-drug addict. I ask the two young men where she was, and they said that they left her in the church parlor with another friend hoping I could help them out. I was a bit skeptical and afraid of what others in town and in my church would think about the main line church pastor dealing with this sort of ministry. It is a taboo subject in the mainline Protestant world. Since she was already in the Parlor, I did not have much of a choice. I went in and talked to the young lady and heard her life story. We talked about the need for her to do some forgiveness work. I asked her to ask God for forgiveness for the wrongs she did to others, rebuking in Jesus' name past activities that were not of God. When we were talking about rebuking bad activities in Jesus' name, the demon revealed himself to me and took over the body. The men had to hold the woman down while I rebuked the demon and demanded him to allow the woman to speak. He did after much prayer and rebuking. When the woman came to her senses, I told her to rebuke quickly her past bad behavior in Jesus' name and to ask for forgiveness. She did and the demon re-appeared. I ordered the demon out because he no longer had any stronghold in the young woman's life and he left. When she came to, she was a different person, loving, kind, healed, and became actively involved in church. We did send her to counseling to continue her forgiveness work and to work through some anger issues, but she was normal and well adjusted as could be.

Some people are not possessed they are oppressed. Oppression and possession are two classifications of demon influence and harassment toward human beings. Demons can influence human beings in many ways.

In demonic oppression, the demon does not directly attack the person but affects his/her behavior and the person's entire life. The person under demonic oppression might display abnormal changes in disposition, attitude, and manners. Even with demonic influence, the person retains control over his or her physical body and mind.

On the other side, demonic possession is the state where the demon gains full command of an individual's body. The demon takes away the person's ability to use his/her physical body, will, consciousness, and freedom. The body adopts the personality, voice, and actions of the demon. By using the person's body, the demon talks to other people by using a different voice and in ways like shouting profanity and taunts. A demon-possessed person can function like a functional drunk and only manifest itself in the presence of the move of the Holy Spirit.

Demonic oppression and possession can be remedied by repenting for past bad behavior and doing forgiveness work in Jesus' name.[9]

It is imperative that we remember that when we encounter evil influences, the only means of being free from the snares of the evil one is to be in alliance with Jesus and His Kingdom. Luke 11:24-26:

- "When an evil spirit comes out of a man, it goes through arid places seeking rest and does not find it. Then it says, 'I will return to the house I left.' When it arrives, it finds the house swept clean and put in order. Then it goes and takes seven other spirits more wicked than itself, and they go in and live there. And the final condition of that man is worse than the first." (NIV)

Throughout the Gospels, especially in Mark and Luke, Jesus has authority over demons, and this proves that He not only is the Son of God but that a new Kingdom is at hand that overcomes the kingdoms and darkness of this world. There was an accusation placed upon Jesus by the religious leaders accusing him of casting out demons in the name of Satan, the prince of all the demons. (Matt. 12:24) There is a hierarchy in the demonic realm and demons can cast out other demonic underlings. There are other people who are occultists or follow false gods or priests for these evil creatures (that are demonic manifestations) that have demonic cohorts in their lives that can perform these supposed feats of power. However, these are not lasting results because only the Kingdom of God and those who follow Jesus can actually cast out demons through the authority of Jesus. That is why it is important to include the statement "in Jesus' name."

So those that seek out help for their demonic possession or oppression from non-Christian sources have a high potential of being a whole lot worse off because seven demons more wicked than the first will come and inhabit them. So it is vital that people accept Jesus as the Messiah and the Son of God in order to overcome the evil that is attacking them. It is also imperative to get involved in a Christian fellowship, small group and continue with Christian counseling.

What Kingdom work is God calling you to do for Him?

When have you seen God work in ways that defeated evil?

Let's pray for success:

> "Almighty God, Who delivered Your people from the bondage of the adversary, and through Your Son cast down Satan like lightning, deliver me also from every influence of unclean spirits. Command Satan to depart far from me by the power of Your only begotten Son. Rescue me from demonic imaginings and darkness. Fill me with the light of the Holy Spirit that I may be guarded against all snares of crafty demons. Grant that an angel will always go before me and lead me to the path of righteousness all the days of my life, to the honor of Your glorious Name, Father, Son and Holy Spirit, now and forever. Amen."[10]

5

ROARING LIONS

"Do not be despondent when fighting against the incorporeal enemy, but even in the midst of your afflictions and oppression praise the Lord, Who has found you worthy to suffer for Him, by struggling against the subtlety of the serpent, and to be wounded for Him at every hour; for had you not lived piously, and endeavored to become united to God, the enemy would not have attacked and tormented you." --John of Kronstadt

- 1 Peter 5:8-9 "Stay alert! Watch out for your great enemy, the devil. He prowls around like a roaring lion, looking for someone to devour. Stand firm against him, and be strong in your faith. Remember that your Christian brothers and sisters all over the world are going through the same kind of suffering you are. (NLT)
- 1 Peter 5:10-11 "In his kindness God called you to share in his eternal glory by means of Christ Jesus. So after you have suffered a little while, he will restore, support, and strengthen you, and he will place you on a firm foundation. All power to him forever! Amen. (NLT)

When I read this passage, I wonder if Peter was reflecting back on that time in his life when he could not stay awake when his best friend and Savior, Jesus, was praying in agony in the Garden of Gethsemane (see Matt 26:36-46).

I love the way Peter tells it like it is. He calls Satan "your enemy the devil" and likens him to a lion in search of prey. The way a lion attacks is by singling out a lone animal that has wandered away from the flock. They choose animals that are not alert and are preoccupied with meeting their desires of eating and not looking up, smelling, or listening to dangerous sounds around them such as rustling grass. Lions will also be able to detect those that are sick, young, and old.

Peter uses this illustration to advise us to be on the lookout for our life long nemesis, Satan. Satan will attack us in the form of suffering, persecution, bullying, mobbing, finances, health and personal attacks by toxic people. When we choose to isolate ourselves, wander off from Christian fellowship, be distracted by worry, are not rested up and overworked and overburdened we forget to watch out for evil; that is when we are the most vulnerable to Satan's attacks.

When you are under spiritual attack, go to your Christian friends for prayer, confession, and support. And as James says: "Submit yourselves, then, to God. Resist the devil, and he will flee from you." James 4:7 (NIV)

I also wonder when Peter said, "Be sober, be watchful" (1 Peter 5:8 ESV) that, once again, it could reflect Peter's experience in which Satan had singled him out for attack because he had failed to watch and be aware of his enemy.

The Christian answer to demonic opposition is not confusion or retreat but firm resistance in faith. We are to struggle against hostile spiritual forces with our positive faith and trust in God. I would like us to focus on one of the most famous stories in the Bible, Daniel in the Den of Lions from Daniel 6:1-28. To understand how Daniel ended up in the lion's den, we have to look at the treacherous and deceitful story that took place when Darius, the Mede was in charge of Babylon. Darius became king because Daniel was able to interpret the writing on the wall at King Belshazzar's party. Belshazzar was slain that very night. So now Darius the Mede received the kingdom. The first thing the king does is reorganize his kingdom and he does this by setting up one hundred and twenty leaders to supervise the kingdom, and three governors to manage the leaders. The reason the new king did this is found in verse 2, so that "the king might not suffer loss."

Right off the bat, we have insight into the character of this king. He is not reorganizing the structure of the kingdom for the benefit of the people so that there will be a greater administration of justice, or so that the place would be so well organized that they could eradicate corruption and poverty. He is appointing those people for his benefit--to protect his properties. This new king is greedy. He has an ego as big as his palace.

Now, one of the three people who take care of King Darius business is Daniel. Because Daniel has distinguished himself with exceptional qualities, the king plans to make him the number one man running the country. Daniel was going to be the right hand of the king. This made everyone else so green with envy that they immediately started plotting a way to get rid of Daniel.

They try to find fault with Daniel. The Bible tells us that he was faithful. No slackness or corruption could be found in him, and those people looked real hard to find something that would take Daniel out. After all of their diabolical scheming, the only way they could find to attack Daniel was to entrap him through his devotion to his one true God. So they concoct a conspiracy based upon Daniel's consistent prayer time. They start out by buttering up King Darius. They say: "O king, live forever. We have got a fantastic idea. You are such a great man that we want to honor you in a very special way. We think it would be wonderful to write a thirty-day law that forbids everybody in the kingdom, under the law of the Medes and the Persians, which are irrevocable, that instead of praying to their gods they should pray to you." Now they slather on the butter saying: "We are going to make you God for thirty days." Now let me just say that this is a hoot. If you are God, you are God forever. But they are going to make King Darius God for a month. Again to the original Jewish audience, this story was so ridiculous, it was hilarious to make this king the Baskin Robbins ice cream flavorful god of the month by simply passing a law and getting the king's signature.

Now we learn that not only is King Darius greedy, he is also extremely vain. We might even add the word gullible because King Darius signed the document not thinking about the consequences of this irrevocable law. There were no questions asked. He just signs the document—and poof he is god for a month.

Daniel is in the hot seat again. He continued to go to his house, which had windows in his upper room opened toward Jerusalem, and to get down on his knees three times a day to pray to his God and praise him, just as he had done previously. The question we need to ponder is: Was Daniel bold and courageous, and consistent with his spiritual commitments, or is he foolhardy and stupid, and is he trying to force the hand of God?

It is my belief that Daniel was aware that if he does not pray to his God, he joins in the idolatry that was prevailing in the land of the people worshiping King Darius as god. So Daniel decides that he is going to be loyal to God and pray anyway. The masterminds of this scheme to kill Daniel knew that they had nothing on him to trap him except for his loyalty to God; so while he was facing in the direction of Jerusalem praying they catch him defying the king's manipulated law to pray to no one else but the thirty days god Darius.

They take their evidence, and they bring it to the king. They say, "You see, he is not praying to you. He is praying to his God. And you have said that anybody who does that will be punished by being thrown in the lion's den." And, of course, the king was very troubled. So in addition to being egocentric, greedy, and gullible, we can also say that King Darius is also a wimp, because he tries everything to save Daniel, but he cannot. His signature on a law that cannot be changed holds the king captive.

Now I am thinking to myself, King Darius, if you are god for thirty days, then why not use your god power to make an exception for your most prized slave named Daniel? God Darius is worthless and inept. So the king commits Daniel to be thrown into the den of lions. And then he says sorrowfully, "May your God, whom you faithfully serve, deliver you." So King Darius, who is god for a month, hopes that the one true God will deliver Daniel.

The king is terrified that Daniel is going to be eaten by lions, all because he chose to sign a stupid law that made him god for thirty days. Darius knows, very well, that he is only playing God. He knows he is just as mediocre as anyone else in the kingdom, and that the real God is going to get after him just like he did King Belshazzar before him. Not only that, King Darius is afraid of the reaction of Daniel's God on his entire kingdom. Daniel is thrown to the lions, and the king went to his palace and spent the night sleeplessly fasting.

Early in the morning we are told the king got up and hurried to the den of lions. A running king is very strange and not normal. A king never does that. A king does not rush anywhere. He always remains majestic and resplendent. He does not get ruffled. But here, he makes a beeline to the lion's den, because he is anxious. He is anxious for himself, as much as for Daniel. King Darius' faith depends on the faith of Daniel.

So we find King Darius crying out, "Oh Daniel, servant of the living God, has your God, whom you faithfully serve, because you serve him, been able to deliver you from the lions?" And he waits for a sound. So Daniel, who is still alive at the bottom of the den, cries out to the king, "O king, live forever!"

This part of the story lets us all know that Daniel is an incredible man of God. Daniel is more of a righteous man than I am. Because, if it had been me in those circumstances I do not know if I would have yelled back: "O king, live forever!" But Daniel is a righteous man and trusts God to make all things right. He even uses this moment to give glory to God by saying: "My God sent his angel to shut the lions' mouths so that they would not hurt me, for I have been found innocent in his sight. And I have not wronged you, Your Majesty." And, of course, the king was exceedingly glad.

All of a sudden King Darius experiences a great transformation because all of a sudden he ceases being a wimp. The king gave a command that those one hundred and twenty-two men who had accused Daniel of betrayal were now going to face the punishment that they gave Daniel. Scripture says: "Then the king gave orders to arrest the men who had maliciously accused Daniel. He had them thrown into the lions' den, along with their wives and children. The lions leaped on them and tore them apart before they even hit the floor of the den."

The king's transformation continues. He says, "May you all have abundant prosperity." He is not talking about his interests and protecting his assets anymore. But this time everybody is supposed to share in the prosperity. Then he dares give a sermon about the living God—the God of Daniel—who can rescue people from the den of lions. Daniel prospered during the reign of King Darius and the reign of Cyrus the Persian.

I believe there are some valuable lessons here for all of us engaged in spiritual warfare, not only for Daniel's period but also for us modern folks. First, all of us believers live in a state of tension between the now and not yet. This world is ruled by the evil system of humanism where many of us mere mortals believe we can save the world and ourselves.

Christian believers live by the fact that we inhabit a God-centered world, not a humanistic centered world. God is at the center. If we view God as the center of the world, that makes an enormous difference on how we see the world, how we view life and the decisions we make. As a result, there is a separation, because Christians cannot identify with a system that exalts humans—in the place of God.

That ideology comes from the fall. Remember when the tempter came to Adam and Eve and said, "You shall be like God," and they fell for it? So there is a very marked difference between being God-centered and humanity centered. The second lesson is not to be anti-cultural, and say: "We belong with God, society does not, and therefore, we are anti-culture." If we are anti-cultural, then we are separated from the world, which should be our mission field. Remember John Wesley said the "world is my parish." The lesson here is Christians should not be anti-cultural, but counter-cultural. They should be part of their culture, to present the Divine alternative to a human-bound world system.

The third lesson plays on the first. In order to offer the Divine alternative, the Christian, by necessity, has to remain distinctive. There is no sense for the Christian believer to join the crowd, and then claim faith. Now for Daniel, the distinctiveness was to keep his nose clean, to remain righteous, and to do his religious duties—to pray three times a day, and so on. What does it mean for us in the New Testament? How shall we be known? What characteristic distinguishes us from others? What is the mark of Christian integrity in the New Testament? It is the law of love. The law of love takes precedence over everything. In fact, Jesus said to "love your neighbor", summarizing all the precepts of the Old Testament.

It also says very clearly in our Bible that love is expressed to people through outreach—outreach in concern, not only for their souls but also for the poor. When we strive for that kind of love, what can we expect? Well, because of the conflict between the two systems of God-centered thinking and humanistic thinking, you can expect a clash, an opposition, and the lion's den.

The message of the Book of Daniel is that we have a God who can deliver. Just as he delivered saints in the old covenant, including

Daniel here from the lion's den, God can deliver us today. But unfortunately for us, if prosperity is a blessing of the Old Testament, adversity is the blessing of the New Testament. Adversity is the blessing because we all know that deliverance is not automatic, and it is not God's obligation. Adversity will happen to believers. Sometimes we will cry for deliverance, and there will be no answer. This was true for Jesus. He met with adversity. And eventually, he was reduced to crying out, "My God, my God, why hast thou forsaken me?" (Matt. 27:46 KJV)

Our Scriptures tell us that we should "consider him, who endured such hostility against himself from sinners so that you may not lose heart" (Heb. 12:3 NLT), because the same thing is going to happen to you. It happened to the Apostles—to the early Christian church, and we even experience it today. According to tradition, the Apostles were all martyred. They all died for the cause of Christ. The Apostle Paul, who was delivered many times from great dangers, eventually put his head on the executioner's block, and he was beheaded. And the early Christians were taken by the Romans and thrown in the middle of the arena, and lions prowled around them trying to decide where they were going to begin their feast. In fact, many of us know that to be true in our own lives. Some of us are struggling with lions within— that are gnawing at our soul and trying to destroy us bit by bit. Sometimes, the lions assail the body; those dreaded diseases that we do not even want to name from fear they will overwhelm us. There seems to be no deliverance. Sometimes the lions are in our social environment, where we experience disdain, rejection, envy, revenge, abandonment, solitude and collective evil.

There are lions all around. Remember Stephen the first martyr. He went before the Supreme Court of his time. Acts 7:54 says:

"When the members of the Sanhedrin heard these things, they became enraged and gnashed their teeth at Stephen." (NIV) You see the lions here? The lions are around, and they are going to try to devour you, but look at Acts 7:55-56: "Filled with the Holy Spirit, he *(Stephen)* gazed into heaven and saw the glory of God and Jesus standing at the right hand of God. 'Look,' he said, 'I see the heavens open and the Son of Man standing at the right hand of God.'" (NIV)

The lions were about to kill him, but he was not alone because Christ was with him. Daniel had an angel muzzle the mouth of the lions. Stephen has it better. He has the presence of Christ himself. And when lions surround us, and they begin to devour us, the greatest comfort, the greatest strength, and the most excellent resource can be the realization that Jesus is right there with us. Jesus has been through it before, and he is with us. There is nothing like suffering to refine our spiritual lives, to improve our character when that suffering is committed for honoring God. Whenever you face trials of any kind, the Word of God says: "Consider it pure joy, my brothers, whenever you face trials of many kinds, because you know that the testing of your faith develops perseverance." (James 1: 2-3 NIV)

And then, there is another lesson. In God's economy, somehow, the greatest advances, the greatest kingdom advances, come through suffering. It was true when Jesus died. It was true at critical phases of the history of the church. The day when Stephen was killed, when the lions finally got him—a severe persecution began against the church in Jerusalem. And as a result, they were scattered throughout the country of Judea. Do you see the sequence here? Jerusalem, Judea, and Samaria. What a command of Christ could not get them to do, the suffering of Stephen and the persecution that ensued finally got them to do. They finally broke loose from Jerusalem and established a church in Judea and Samaria, and then had further conquest of the world.

The Church was freed by persecution, to do what Christ had wanted it to do. I am sure many of you can point to some experience where you have learned things that you would have never learned if it had not been for the hardship, for the adversity, for the fact that the lions were around, and they seemed to get the better of you. But then, God used that very circumstance to bring a blessing that could have come in no other way, which is better than any other deliverance that you might have expected. Many of us know from our personal suffering; on one hand, there was suffering, but on the other hand, God, out of that suffering, brought a blessing that could not have come any other way.

"Be alert and of sober mind. Your enemy the devil prowls around like a roaring lion looking for someone to devour." 1 Peter 5:8 (NIV) Do not forget that the idea here is there is a group of Christians huddled in the arena, and somebody is going to go first. All you can do is resist and stand steadfast in your faith, for you know that your brothers and sisters all around the world are undergoing the same kind of suffering. There will be suffering.

Hear the good news: "And the God of all grace, who called you to his eternal glory in Christ, after you have suffered a little while, will himself restore you and make you strong, firm and steadfast." (1 Peter 5:10 NIV) The good news of this scriptural promise is that when we go through a spiritual battle and get clobbered, God will restore what Satan stole. God will strengthen us when we are weak as a kitten after a rough battle that we fought or lost. God will make us resolute once again. Peter encouraged his readers to endure suffering and spiritual attacks in such a way that the grace of God would be made evident in their lives.

Do you realize you are a target?

When were you attacked?

Have you had anyone scheme against you to take you out?

Have you had anyone jealous of you and your accomplishments?

Do you believe in supernatural intervention to keep the mouths of the lions closed in your life?

Have you ever been vindicated?

If not, how do you deal with the injustice?

Look up Psalm 59 and read it as a prayer for your life. This psalm is a prayer that David prayed for deliverance from bloodthirsty men. David trusted God for his defense and to keep him safe from his enemies.

6

GROUND ZERO THE BATTLE WITH THE FLESH

"Faith, without trouble or fighting, is a suspicious faith; for true faith is a fighting, wrestling faith." --Ralph Erskine

I have heard people say they have a body with a soul in it. I say we have a soul that is using a temporal body. This second approach helps us to understand that we are spiritual beings and that our body is just temporary because we are waiting for a new resurrected body that is going to be awesome! It can walk through walls, transport us from one place to another, we can still eat, but this body will not age, rot, or get sick or hurt. But, until that day, we must battle the flesh of this temporal body until the perfect one comes. We have to remember that Satan wants to attack this body and use it to destroy us. So we must do some soul searching within our hearts and minds to overcome our personal attacks. I called this chapter "Ground Zero" because we are going to look at how to overcome the war between our body and our soul.

We were created in the image of God and God even said, after he created man and woman, that it was good. So the flesh is not bad, it is falling into temptation and allowing the temptation to manifest itself. When this manifestation happens, it will take control over our body, motives, mind, heart, and being. The sinful desires of our flesh go all the way back to the story of the Garden of Eden.

In our society today, the only sin in the world is to say that there is no sin. Sin, in its simplest definition, is disobedience of God's law (the Ten Commandments) and rebellion against God. This can also include more specifically any action that injures the relationship we have with God or another person. It is to make a deliberate choice to participate in bad behavior that disconnects us from God. God created us to be in a relationship with Him. To maintain this relationship, not only do we need to make time for him in prayer, Bible study, worship and theological reflection, we must also be in a covenant relationship with God's laws both spiritual and natural. Sin is anything that gets in the way of our relationship with God.

It takes belief in Jesus as our Savior to break Adam's curse. Sin arrived to our world when Adam ate from the tree of knowledge and evil. God had forbidden this so all of us have inherited a "sin nature" from Adam. We are basically born with a bent toward sinning. We are all born with a predisposition to reject God. So let's look at this inherited disposition that is bent on sinning and try to understand the nature behind the "desires of the flesh" or the "nature within us" in order to be battle ready.

I love how Paul describes it: "I don't really understand myself, for I want to do what is right, but I don't do it. Instead, I do what I hate. (Romans 7:15 NLT)

Paul was confessing that he did not know why he was practicing the bad behavior that he knew was wrong. Our actions are at the directive of someone or something external to ourselves to the point that we, like Paul, sometimes have no clue as how to explain it. Paul said: "For what I wish to do I am not doing. That which I hate to do I am doing!"

To understand what is going on, we need to look at the theological concept of Sanctification. My favorite and least complicated definition comes from St. Augustine: "God made me good but not yet." John Wesley believed that the Methodist understanding of Sanctification was the best gift to Christianity. He defined it this way in one of his sermons: "It is thus that we wait for entire sanctification; for a full salvation from all our sins, from pride, self-will, anger, unbelief; or, as the Apostle expresses it, 'go on unto perfection.'" [11]

But what is perfection? The word has various senses: here it means perfect love. It is love excluding sin, love filling the heart, love taking up the whole capacity of the soul. It is love "rejoicing evermore, praying without ceasing, in every thing giving thanks." Wesley goes on to preach in the same sermon: "I have continually testified in private and in public, that we are sanctified as well as justified by faith. And indeed the one of those great truths does exceedingly illustrate the other. Exactly as we are justified by faith, so are we sanctified by faith. Faith is the condition, and the only condition, of sanctification, exactly as it is of justification. It is the condition: None is sanctified but he that believes; without faith no man is sanctified. And it is the only condition: This alone is sufficient for sanctification. Every one that believes is sanctified, whatever else he has or has not. In other words, no man is sanctified till he believes: Every man when he believes is sanctified." [12]

Basically, Sanctification and Justification are the two sides of one coin. Jesus frees us from Sin and makes us holy (Sanctification) and then, on the other side of the coin, we are Justified and made right with God and judged worthy of being a child of God because of Jesus' sacrifice on the cross and our belief that Jesus is God's son. We are constantly battling between what we want to do and what God wants us to do. But no matter what, we are saved by grace through faith. We strive toward perfect love and aim for the goal of being holy like God is Holy, knowing that when we fail we can ask for forgiveness, knock the dust off, get back up and carry on, learning from our mistakes.

Paul in Galatians 5:16-17 unpacks it this way for us:

- "So I say, walk by the Spirit, and you will not gratify the desires of the flesh. For the flesh desires what is contrary to the Spirit, and the Spirit what is contrary to the flesh. They are in conflict with each other, so that you are not to do whatever you want." (NIV)

So as a believer we are supposed to "keep on keeping on" and allow the Holy Spirit to inhabit us. The Holy Spirit is not the simplification of guidance but helps us with the power to overcome our "flesh" and "the world." It is imperative that we work on allowing the Holy Spirit not only to be present in our lives but also to allow Him to be President of our lives by yielding to His control. This is the only way we can overcome the desires of our sinful nature. While no believer will ever be entirely free in this life from the evil desires that stem from his/her fallen human nature, he/she does not need to surrender to them, but rather rely on the Holy Spirit's help to experience victory.

Paul taught that we have two natures, a sinful nature inherited from the fall received at birth, and a new nature received when we accepted Christ. Both of our natures have strong desires, one for evil and the other for holiness. They wage war in our lives because they are in conflict with each other. All I can say is, thank God for grace! We cannot achieve sanctification, or justification for that matter, by our own human determination. The only way we can strive toward holiness is by placing our faith in Christ to save us and in the Holy Spirit to sanctify us!

Since I have daughters, we rarely use up our half-gallon of milk before it spoils. I talk to families with sons and hear that they go through two gallons a week! So when I go to the store, I never get the first half-gallon off the shelf. I reach in the back and find one with the latest expiration date so I can try to use as much as possible before it spoils. God's grace and love do not have an expiration date! It is always available to those who seek God! This grace never spoils and never runs out! That is God's amazing grace that is available to anyone who would seek out salvation through Jesus Christ.

Can you relate to the struggle Paul is talking about?

Do you ever get down on yourself for doing what you know is wrong?

What are some "tug of war" situations you have faced with your own personal dual natures?

How can you let Go and let God lead?

How can you strive towards perfect love?

Pray to be filled with the Holy Spirit. Allow the Holy Spirit to not only be present in your life but to be President of your life as you learn to follow God's leading.

Pray the following (Greek Orthodox Prayer):

Exalted Creator, I bless Your holy name. We give You all the praise, honor and glory You deserve, for You are Holy and Righteous. I come before You, gentle Savior, seeking Your help in battling temptations. Cleanse my mind, my body, my soul, of all lustful desires. Deliver me from the evil one, Yahweh, protect me from his deceitful lies.

Aid me in becoming righteous, pure and holy. Help me not to be consumed by thoughts of lust. Let my mind focus on praising and worshiping You and You alone, for my body is a temple of the Holy Ghost. I bind and curse out every evil entity that prevents me from building a closer relationship between us; lust, adultery, fornication, lasciviousness, and sexual immorality.

The only thing I crave, hunger and thirst after is You Jehovah Nissi. Almighty God, Everlasting Father, I know

You will help me through this. I may be human, which makes me weak at times, but I will not yield to temptation, for yielding is sin because I am strong through Christ who gives me strength. Satan shall not prevail! The works of the wicked shall not prosper, for we are healed, delivered and saved, through the Father, the Son and the Holy Spirit, Amen and Amen[13]

7

OF GOOD ANGELS

I have included in this book two sermons written/preached by John Wesley. I will attempt to ask provocative questions at the beginning of each sermon to try to help you think theologically as you read through the text about good and evil angels that affect our lives. I have also updated the sermons from old English to modern English while still keeping the original intent of the elusive Rev. John Wesley.

According to Wesley do angels know what we are thinking and what concerns and fears we have?

Does Wesley's view of angels change your attitude toward the supernatural war that rages around us?

What kind of power do angels have to employ on our behalf?

How do angels minister to us?

How do angels protect us?

Of Good Angels
John Wesley

"Are not all angels ministering spirits sent to serve those who will inherit salvation?" --Hebrews 1:14 (NKJV)

Many of the ancient Heathens had (probably from tradition) some notion of good and evil angels. They had some conception of a superior order of beings, between men and God, whom the Greeks generally termed demons, (knowing ones,) and the Romans, genii. Some of these they supposed to be kind and benevolent, delighting in doing good; others, to be malicious and cruel, delighting in doing evil. But their conceptions both of one and the other were crude, imperfect, and confused; being only fragments of truth, partly delivered down by their forefathers, and partly borrowed from the inspired writings.

Of the former, the benevolent kind seems to have been the celebrated demon of Socrates; concerning which so many and so various conjectures have been made in succeeding ages. "This gives me notice," said he, "every morning, of any evil that will befall me that day." A late writer, indeed, (I suppose one that hardly believes the existence of either angel or spirit,) has published a dissertation, wherein he labors to prove, that the demon of Socrates was only his reason. But it was not the manner of Socrates to speak in such obscure and ambiguous terms. If he had meant his reason, he would doubtless have said so. But this could not be his meaning: For it was impossible, his reason should give him notice, every morning, of every evil that would befall him in that day. It does not lie within the province of reason, to give such notice of future contingencies. Neither does this odd interpretation in anywise agree with the inference that he draws from it. "My demon," says he, "did not give me notice this morning of any evil that was to befall me to-day. Therefore, I cannot regard as any evil my being condemned to die." Undoubtedly it was some spiritual being: Probably one of these ministering spirits.

An ancient poet, one who lived several ages before Socrates, speaks more determinately on this subject. Hesiod does not scruple to say, Millions of spiritual creatures walk the earth unseen. Therefore, it is probable, arose the numerous tales about the exploits of their demi-gods: Minorum Gentium. Hence their satyrs, fauns, nymphs of every kind; wherewith they supposed both the sea and land to be filled. But how empty, childish, unsatisfactory, are all the accounts they give of them! As, indeed, accounts that depend upon broken, uncertain tradition can hardly fail to be.

Revelation only can supply this defect: This only gives us a clear, rational, consistent account of those whom our eyes have not seen, nor our ears heard; of both good and evil angels. It is my design to speak, at present, only of the former; of whom we have a full, though brief account in these words: "Are they not all ministering spirits, sent forth to minister unto them that shall be heirs of salvation?"

The question is, according to the manner of the Apostle, equivalent to a strong affirmation. And therefore we learn, First, that concerning their essence, or nature, they are all spirits; not material beings; not clogged with flesh and blood like us; but having bodies, if any, not gross and earthly like ours, but of a finer substance; resembling fire or flame, more than any other of these lower elements. And is not something like this intimated in those words of the Psalmist: "Who makes his angels spirits, and his ministers a flame of fire?" (Psalm 104:4.) As spirits, he has endued them with understanding, will, or affections, (which are indeed the same thing; as the affections are only the will exerting itself various ways,) and liberty. And are not these, understanding, will, and liberty, essential to, if not the essence of, a spirit?

But who of the children of men can comprehend what is the understanding of an angel? Who can comprehend how far their sight extends? Analogous to sight in men, though not the same; but thus we are constrained to speak through the poverty of human language. Probably not only over one hemisphere of the earth; yea, or, Ten-fold the length of this terrene; or even of the solar system; but so far as to take in one view the whole extent of the creation! And we cannot conceive any defect in their perception; neither any error in their understanding. But in what manner do they use their understanding? We must in nowise imagine that they creep from one truth to another by that slow method that we call reasoning. Undoubtedly they see, at one glance, whatever truth is presented to their understanding; and that with all the certainty and clearness that we mortals see the most self-evident axiom. Who then can conceive the extent of their knowledge? Not only of nature, attributes, and works of God, whether of creation or providence; but of the circumstances, actions, words, tempers, yea, and thoughts, of men. For although "God" only "knows the hearts of all men," ("unto whom are known all his works,") together with the changes they undergo, "from the beginning of the world;" yet we cannot doubt but his angels know the hearts of those to whom they more immediately minister. Much less can we doubt of their knowing the thoughts that are in our hearts at any particular time. What should hinder their seeing them as they arise? Not the thin veil of flesh and blood. Can these intercept the view of a spirit? No, walls within walls no more its passage bar, Than unimposing space of liquid air. Far more easily, then, and far more perfectly, than we can read a man's thoughts in his face, do these sagacious beings read our thoughts just as they rise in our hearts; since they see the kindred spirit, more clearly than we see the body. If this seems strange to any who had not adverted to it before, let him only consider: Suppose my spirit was out of the body, could not an angel see my thoughts, even without my uttering any words? (if words are used in the world of spirits.) And cannot that ministering spirit see them just as well now that I am in the body? It seems, therefore, to be unquestionable truth, (although perhaps not commonly observed,) that angels know not only the words and actions but also the thoughts, of those to whom they minister. And indeed without this knowledge, they would be very ill qualified to perform various parts of their ministry.

And what an inconceivable degree of wisdom must they have acquired by the use of their amazing faculties, over and above that with which they were originally endued, in the course of more than six thousand years! (That they have existed so long we are assured; for they "sang together when the foundations of the earth were laid.") How immensely must their wisdom have increased, during so long a period, not only by surveying the hearts and ways of men in their successive generations, but by observing the works of God, his works of creation, his works of providence, his works of grace; and, above all, by "continually beholding the face of their Father which is in heaven!"

What measures of holiness, as well as wisdom, have they derived from this inexhaustible ocean! A boundless, fathomless abyss, without a bottom or a shore! Are they not therefore, by way of eminence, styled the holy angels? What goodness, what philanthropy, what love to man, have they drawn from those rivers that are at his right hand! Such as we cannot conceive to be exceeded by any but that of God our Savior. And they are still drinking in more love from this "Fountain of living water."

Such is the knowledge and wisdom of the angels of God, as we learn from his oracles. Such are their holiness and goodness. And how astonishing is their strength! Even a fallen angel is styled by an inspired writer, "the prince of the power of the air." How terrible a proof did he give of this power, in suddenly raising the whirlwind, which "smote the four corners of the house," and destroyed all the children of Job at once! (Job 1.) That this was his work, we may easily learn from the command to "save his life." But he gave a far more terrible proof of his strength, (if we suppose that "messenger of the Lord" to have been an evil angel, as is not at all improbable,) when he smote with death a hundred, eighty five thousand Assyrians in one night; indeed, possibly in one hour, if not one moment. A strength abundantly greater than this must have been exerted by that angel (whether he was an angel of light or darkness; which is not determined by the text) who smote, in one hour, "all the first-born of Egypt, both of man and beast." For, considering the extent of the land of Egypt, the immense population, and the innumerable cattle fed in their houses, and grazing in their fruitful fields; the men and beasts who were slain in that night must have amounted to several million! And if this is supposed to have been an evil angel, must not a good angel be as strong, yea, stronger than him? For surely any good angel must have more power than even an archangel ruined. And what power must the "four angels" in the Revelation have, who were appointed to "keep the four winds of heaven!" There seems, therefore, no extravagance in supposing, that, if God were pleased to permit, any of the angels of light could hurl the earth and all the planets out of heir orbits; certainly, that he could arm himself with all these elements, and crush the whole frame of nature. Indeed, we do not know how to set any bounds to the strength of these first-born children of God.

And although none but their great Creator is omnipresent; although none beside him can ask, "Do not I fill heaven and earth?" Undoubtedly, he has given an immense sphere of action (though not unbounded) to created spirits. "The prince of the kingdom of Persia," (mentioned Dan. 10:13,) though probably an evil angel, seems to have had a sphere of action, both of knowledge and power, as extensive as that vast empire; and the same, if not greater, we may reasonably ascribe to the good angel whom he withstood for one-and-twenty days.

The angels of God have great power, in particular, over the human body; power either to cause or remove pain and diseases, either to kill or to heal. They perfectly well understand of which we are made; they know all the springs of this curious machine, and can, doubtless, by God's permission, touch any of them, so as either to stop or restore its motion. Of this power, even in an evil angel, we have a clear instance in the case of Job; whom he "smote with sore boils" all over, "from the crown of the head to the sole." And in that instant, undoubtedly, he would have killed him, if God had not saved his life. And, on the other hand, of the power of angels to heal, we have a remarkable instance in the case of Daniel. There remained no "strength in me," said the prophet; "neither was there breath in me." "Then one came and touched me, and said, Peace be unto thee: Be strong, yea, be strong. And when he had spoken unto me, I was strengthened." (Dan. 10:17.) On the other hand, when they are commissioned from above, may they not put a period to human life? There is nothing improbable in what Dr. Parnell supposes the angel to say to the hermit, concerning the death of the child: -- To all but thee, in fits he seemed to go:

And it was my ministry to deal the blow. From this great truth, the heathen poets probably derived their imagination, that Iris used to be sent down from heaven to discharge souls out of their bodies. And perhaps the sudden death of many of the children of God may be owing to the ministry of an angel.

So perfectly are the angels of God qualified for their high office. It remains to inquire, how they discharge their office. How do they minister to the heirs of salvation?

I will not say, that they do not minister at all to those who, through their obstinate impenitence and unbelief, disinherit themselves of the kingdom. This world is a world of mercy, wherein God pours down many mercies, even on the evil and the unthankful. And many of these, it is probable, are conveyed even to them by the ministry of angels; especially, so long as they have any thought of God or any fear of God before their eyes. But it is their favorite employ, their peculiar office, to minister to the heirs of salvation; to those who are now "saved by faith," or at least seeking God in sincerity.

Is it not their first care to minister to our souls? But we must not expect this will be done with observation; in such a manner, as that we may clearly distinguish their working from the workings of our minds. We have no more reason to look for this, than for their appearing in a visible shape. Without this, they can, in a thousand ways, apply to our understanding. They may assist us in our search after truth, remove many doubts and difficulties, throw light on what was before dark and obscure, and confirm us in the truth that is after godliness. They may warn us of evil in disguise; and place what is good, in a clear, strong light. They may gently move our will to embrace what is good, and fly from that which is evil. They may, many times, quicken our dull affections, increase our holy hope or filial fear, and assist us more ardently to love Him who has first loved us.

Yea, they may be sent of God to answer that whole prayer, put into our mouths by pious Bishop Ken: --

O may thy angels while I sleep,
Around my bed their vigils keep;
Their love angelical instill,
Stop every avenue of ill!
May they celestial joys rehearse,
And thought to thought with me converse!

Although the manner of this we shall not be able to explain while we dwell in the body. May they not also minister to us, on our bodies, in a thousand ways, which we do not now understand? They may prevent our falling into many dangers, which we are not sensible of; and may deliver us out of many others, though we know not whence our deliverance comes. How many times have we been strangely and unaccountably preserved, in sudden and dangerous falls! And it is well if we did not impute that preservation to chance, or to our wisdom or strength. Not so: It was God gave his angels charge over us, and in their hands they bore us up. Indeed, men of the world will always impute such deliverances to accident or second causes. To these, possibly, some of them might have imputed Daniel's preservation in the lion's den. But himself ascribes it to the true cause: "My God has sent his angel, and shut the lions' mouths." (Dan. 6:22.)

When a violent disease, supposed to be incurable, is totally and suddenly removed, it is by no means improbable that this is affected by the ministry of an angel. And perhaps it is owing to the same cause, that a remedy is unaccountably suggested either to the sick person, or some attending upon him, by which he is entirely cured.

It seems, what are usually called divine dreams may be frequently ascribed to angels. We have a remarkable instance of this kind related by one that will hardly be thought an enthusiast; for he was a Heathen, a Philosopher, and an Emperor: I mean Marcus Antoninus. "In his Meditations, he solemnly thanks God for revealing to him, when he was at Cajeta, in a dream, what totally cured the bloody flux; that none of his physicians were able to heal." And why may we not suppose, that God gave him this notice by the ministry of an angel?

And how often does God deliver us from evil men by the ministry of his angels! Overturning whatever their rage, or malice, or elusiveness had plotted against us. These are about their bed, and about their path, and privy to all their dark designs; and many of them, undoubtedly, they brought to naught, by means that we do not think of. Sometimes they blast their favorite schemes in the beginning; sometimes, when they are just ripe for execution. And this they can do by a thousand means that we are not aware of. They can check them in their mid-career, by bereaving them of courage or strength; by striking faintness through their loins, or turning their wisdom into foolishness. Sometimes they bring to light the hidden things of darkness and show us the traps that are laid for our feet. In these and various other ways, they hew the snares of the ungodly in pieces.

Another grand branch of their ministry is, to counterwork evil angels; who are continually going about, not only as roaring lions, seeking whom they may devour but, more dangerously still, as angels of light, seeking whom they may deceive. And how great is the number of these! Are they not as the stars of heaven for multitude? How great is their subtlety! Matured by the experience of above six thousand years. How great is their strength! Only inferior to that of the angels of God. The strongest of the sons of men are but as grasshoppers before them. And what an advantage have they over us by that single circumstance, that they are invisible! As we have not strength to repel their force, so we have not skilled to decline it. But the merciful Lord has not given us up to the will of our enemies: "His eyes," that is, his holy angels, "run to and fro over all the earth." And if our eyes were opened, we should see, "they are more that are for us, than they that are against us." We should see, a convoy attends, a ministering host of invisible friends. And whenever those assault us in soul or the body, these are able, willing, ready, to defend us; who are at least equally strong, equally wise, and equally vigilant. And who can hurt us while we have armies of angels, and the God of angels, on our side?

And we may make one general observation: Whatever assistance God gives to men by men, the same, and frequently in a higher degree, he gives to them by angels. Does he administer to us by men, light when we are in darkness;

joy, when we are in heaviness; deliverance, when we are in danger; ease and health, when we are sick or in pain? It cannot be doubted, but he frequently conveys the same blessings by the ministry of angels: Not so sensibly indeed, but full as effectually; though the messengers are not seen. Does he frequently deliver us, using men, from the violence and subtlety of our enemies? Many times he works the same deliverance by those invisible agents. These shut the mouths of the human lions so that they have no power to hurt us. And frequently they join with our human friends, (although neither they nor we are sensible of it,) giving them wisdom, courage, or strength, which all their labor for us would be unsuccessful. Thus do they secretly minister, in numberless instances, to the heirs of salvation; while we hear only the voices of men, and see none but men around us.

But does not the Scripture teach, "The help that is done upon earth, God does it himself?" Most certainly he does. And he can do it by his own immediate power. He has no need of using any instruments at all, either in heaven or earth. He wants not either angels or men, to fulfill the whole counsel of his will. But it is not his pleasure so to work. He never did, and we may reasonably suppose he never will. He has always wrought by such instruments as he pleases: But still it is God himself that doeth the work. Whatever help, therefore, we have, either by angels or men, is as much the work of God, as if he were to put forth his almighty arm, and work without any means at all. But he has used them from the beginning of the world: In all ages he has used the ministry both of men and angels. And at this moment, especially, is seen "the manifold wisdom of God in the Church." Meantime the same glory redounds to him as if he used no instruments at all.

The grand reason God is pleased to assist men by men, rather than immediately by himself, is undoubted to endear us to each other by these mutual good offices, to increase our happiness both in time and eternity. And is it not for the same reason that God is pleased to give his angels charge over us? Namely, that he may endear us, and them to each other; that by the increase of our love and gratitude to them, we may find a proportional increase of happiness, when we meet in our Father's kingdom. In the meantime, though we may not worship them, (worship is due only to our common Creator,) yet we may "esteem them very highly in love for their works' sake." And we may imitate them in all holiness; suiting our lives to the prayer our Lord himself has taught us; laboring to do his will on earth, as angels do it in heaven.

I cannot conclude this discourse better than in that admirable Collect of our Church: --

"O everlasting God, who hast ordained and constituted the services of angels and men in a wonderful manner; grant that as your holy angels always do your service in heaven, so by thy appointment they may support and defend us on earth, through Jesus Christ our Lord."

8

OF EVIL ANGELS

Here are a few questions to ponder as you read through John Wesley's sermon/teaching on evil angels.

How did angels become evil?

What has God's word revealed to you about evil angels?

What are some of the gifts that evil angels possess?

What do evil angels do to trip us up and harass us?

Do we have a guardian angel assigned to us along with an evil one to wage war against us?

Of Evil Angels
John Wesley

"We wrestle not against flesh and blood, but against principalities, against powers, against the rulers of the darkness of this world, against wicked spirits in heavenly places." --Ephesians 6:12. (KJV)

It has been frequently observed that there are no gaps or chasms in the creation of God, but that all the parts of it are admirably connected, to make up one universal as a whole. Accordingly, there is one chain of beings, from the lowest to the highest point, from an unorganized particle of earth or water to Michael the archangel. And the scale of creatures does not advance per saltum, {Per saltum is a Latin phrase, meaning "hopping." It is used to mean that someone has reached a position or degree without going through the ranks and working their way up. They hopped over everyone else to get to where they are} but by smooth and gentle degrees; although it is true, these are frequently invisible to our imperfect faculties. We cannot accurately trace many of the intermediate links of this amazing chain, which are abundantly too fine to be discerned either by our senses or understanding.

We can only observe, in a whole and general manner, rising one above another, first, inorganically earth, then minerals and vegetables in their several orders; afterward insects, reptiles, fishes, beasts, men, and angels. Of angels indeed we know nothing with any certainty but by revelation. The accounts that are left by the wisest of the ancients, or given by the modern heathens, being no better than silly, self-inconsistent fables, too gross to be imposed even upon children. But by divine revelation we are informed that they were all created holy and happy, yet they did not all continue as they were created: some kept, but some left, their first estate. The former of these are now good angels; the latter, evil angels. Of the former I have spoken in the preceding discourse: I purpose now to speak of the latter. And it is extremely important that we should well understand what God has revealed concerning them, that they may gain no advantage over us by our ignorance; that we may know how to wrestle against them effectually. For "we wrestle not against flesh and blood, but against principalities, against powers, against the rulers of the darkness of this world, against wicked spirits in heavenly places."

This single passage seems to contain the whole scriptural doctrine concerning evil angels. I understand the plain meaning of it, literally translated, is this: "Our wrestling," the wrestling of real Christians, "is not" only, or chiefly, "against flesh and blood," weak men, or fleshly appetites and passions, "but against principalities, against powers," -- the mighty princes of all the infernal regions, with their combined forces: And great is their power, as is also the power of the legions they command, -- "against the rulers of the world" (This is the literal meaning of the word.) Perhaps these principalities and powers remain chiefly in the citadel of their kingdom. But there are other evil spirits that range abroad, to whom the provinces of the world are committed, "of the darkness," chiefly the spiritual darkness, "of this age," which prevails during this present state of things, "against wicked spirits" -- notably; who mortally hate and continually oppose holiness, and labor to infuse unbelief, pride, evil desire, malice, anger, hatred, envy, or revenge – "in heavenly places;" which were once their abode, and which they still aspire after.

In prosecuting this important subject, I will endeavor to explain, the nature and properties of evil angels; and, their employment.

Concerning the First, we cannot doubt but all the angels of God were originally of the same nature. Unquestionably they were the highest order of created beings. They were spirits, pure ethereal creatures, simple and incorruptible; if not wholly immaterial, yet certainly not encumbered with gross, earthly flesh and blood. As spirits, they were endued with understanding, with affections, and with liberty, or a power of self-determination; so that it lay in themselves, either to continue in their allegiance to God or to rebel against him.

Their original characteristics were, surely, the same with those of the holy angels. There is no absurdity in supposing Satan their chief, otherwise styled, "Lucifer, son of the morning," to have been at least one "of the first, if not the first Archangel." Like the other sons of the morning, they had a height and depth of understanding quite incomprehensible to us. In consequence of this they had such knowledge and wisdom, which the wisest of the children of men (had men then existed) would have been mere idiots in comparison of them. Their strength was equal to their knowledge; such as it cannot enter into our heart to conceive; neither can we conceive to how wide a sphere of action either their strength or their knowledge extended or their numbers.

God alone can tell: Doubtless it was only less than infinite. And a third part of these stars of heaven the arch-rebel drew after him.

We do not exactly know, (because it is not revealed in the canons of God,) either what was the occasion of their apostasy, or what affect it immediately produced upon them. Some have, not improbably, supposed, that when God published "the decree" (mentioned Ps. 2:6-7) concerning the kingdom of his only-begotten Son to be over all creatures, these first-born of creatures fell into pride, comparing themselves to him; -- possibly intimated by the very name of Satan, Lucifer, or Michael, which means, Who is like God? It may be, Satan, then first giving way to temptation, said in his heart, "I too will have my throne. I will sit upon the sides of the north! I will be like the Most High.'" How did the mighty fall! What an amazing loss did they sustain! If we allow them all what our poet supposes concerning their chief, in particular, --

His form had not yet lost
All its original brightness, nor appeared
Less than archangel ruined, and the excess
Of glory obscured;

If we suppose their outward form was not entirely changed (though it must have been in a great degree; because the evil disposition of the mind must dim the luster of the visage,) yet what an astonishing change was wrought within when angels became devils! When the holiest of all the creatures of God became the most unholy!

From the time that they shook off their allegiance to God, they shook off all goodness and contracted all those tempers that are most hateful to him, and most opposite to his nature. And ever since they are full of pride, arrogance, haughtiness, exalting themselves above measure; and although so deeply depraved through their inner frame, yet admiring their perfections. They are full of envy, if not against God himself, (and even that is not impossible, seeing they formerly aspired after his throne,) but against all their fellow-creatures; against the angels of God, who now enjoy the heaven from which they fell; and much more against those worms of the earth who are now called to "inherit the kingdom." They are full of cruelty, of rage against all the children of men, whom they long to inspire with the same wickedness with themselves, and to involve in the same misery.

In the prosecution of this infernal design, they are diligent in the highest degree. To find out the most effectual means of putting it into execution, they apply to this end the whole force of their angelical understanding; and they second it with their whole strength, so far as God is pleased to permit. But it is well for humanity that God has set them bounds in which they cannot pass. He has said to the fiercest and strongest of the apostate spirits: "You shall not pass." Otherwise, how easily and how quickly might one of them overturn the whole fabric of nature! How soon would they involve all in one common destruction, or, at least, destroy man from the face of the earth! And they are inexhaustible in their bad work: They never are faint or weary. Indeed, it seems no spirits are capable of weariness but those that inhabit flesh and blood.

One more circumstance we may learn from the Scripture concerning the evil angels: They do not wander at large, but are all united under one common head. It is he that is formed by our blessed Lord, "the prince of this world:" Yea, the Apostle, does not scruple to call him, "the god of this world." He has frequently styled Satan, the adversary; being the great adversary both of God and man. He is termed "the devil," by way of eminence; -- "Apollyon," or the destroyer; -- "the old serpent," from his beguiling Eve under that form; -- and, "the angel of the bottomless pit." We have reason to believe that the other evil angels are under his command; that he ranges them according to their several orders; that they are appointed to their several stations, and have, from time to time, their several works and offices assigned them. And, undoubtedly, they are connected (though we know not how; certainly not by love) both to him and to each other.

But what is the employment of evil angels? This is the Second point to be considered. They are (remember, so far as God permits!) kosmokratores, {Greek for rulers of tis world} --governors of the world! So that there may be more ground than we are apt to imagine for that strange expression of Satan, (Matt. 4:8-9,) when he showed our Lord "all the kingdoms of the world, and the glory of them," "All these things will I give you, if you will fall down and worship me." It is a little more particularly expressed in the fourth chapter of St. Luke: "The devil showed unto him all the kingdoms of the world in a moment of time." (Such an astonishing measure of power is still left in the prince of darkness!) "And the devil said, All this power will I give thee, and the glory of them: For that is delivered unto me; and to whomsoever I will, I give it." (Matt. 4:5, 6,) They are "the rulers of the darkness of this age;" (so the words are translated;) of the present state of things, during which "the whole world is in bed wit the wicked one." He is the element of the children of men; only those who fear God being excepted. He and his angels, in connection with, and in submission to him, dispose of all the ignorance, all the error, all the folly, and particularly all the wickedness of men, in such a manner as may most hinder the kingdom of God, and most advances the kingdom of darkness.

"But has every man a particular evil angel, as well as a good one attending him?" This has been an exceeding ancient opinion, both among the Christians, and the Jews before them: But it is very doubtful whether or not it can be sufficiently proved from Scripture. Indeed, it would not be improbable that there is a particular evil angel with every man if we were convinced there is a good one. But this cannot be inferred from those words of our Lord concerning little children: "In heaven their angels do continually see the face of their Father, which is in heaven." This only proves that there are angels who are appointed to take care of little children: It does not prove that a particular angel is allotted to every child. Neither is it proved by the words of Rhoda, who, hearing the voice of Peter, said, "It is his angel." We cannot infer any more from this, even suppose his angel means his guardian angel than that Rhoda believed the doctrine of guardian angels, which was then common among the Jews. But still it will remain a disputable point, (seeing revelation determines nothing concerning it,) whether every man is attended either by a particular good or a particular evil angel.

But whether or not particular men are attended by particular evil spirits, we know that Satan and all his angels are continually warring against us, and watching over every human child. They are always watching to see whose outward or inward circumstances, whose prosperity or adversity, whose health or sickness, whose friends or enemies, whose youth or age, whose knowledge or ignorance, whose blindness or idleness, whose joy or sorrow, may lay them open to temptation. And they are perpetually ready to make the maximum advantage of every circumstance. These skillful wrestlers spot the smallest slip we make, and avail themselves of it immediately; as they also are "about our bed, and about our path, and spy out all our ways." Indeed each of them "walks about as a roaring lion, seeking whom he may devour," or whom he may "beguile through his subtlety, as the serpent beguiled Eve."

In order to do this the more effectually, they transform themselves into angels of light. Thus, with rage that never ends, their hellish arts they try; Legions of dire, malicious fiends, and spirits enthroned on high.

It is by these instruments chiefly that the "foolish hearts" of those that do not know God "are darkened:" Surely, they frequently darken, in a measure, the hearts of those that do know God. The "god of this world" knows how to blind our hearts, to spread a cloud over our understanding, and to obscure the light of those truths that, at other times, shine as bright as the noonday sun. By this means, he assaults our faith, our evidence of things unseen. He endeavors to weaken that hope full of immortality to which God had given us; and thereby to lessen, if he cannot destroy, our joy in God our Savior. But, above all he strives to cloudy our love of God, as he knows this is the spring of all our religion, and that, as this rises or falls, the work of God flourishes or decays in the soul.

Next to the love of God, there is nothing that Satan so cordially abhors as the love of our neighbor. He uses, therefore, every possible means to prevent or destroy this; to excite either private or public suspicions, animosities, resentment, quarrels; to destroy the peace of families or nations; and to banish unity and concord from the earth. And this, indeed, is the triumph of his art; to embitter the poor, miserable children of men against each other, and at length urge them to do his work, to plunge one another into the pit of destruction.

This enemy of all righteousness is equally diligent to hinder every good word and work. If he cannot prevail upon us to do evil, he will, if possible, prevent our doing good. He is peculiarly diligent to hinder the work of God from spreading in the hearts of men. What pains does he take to prevent or obstruct the general work of God! And how many are his devices to stop its progress in selective souls! To hinder their continuing or growing in grace, in the knowledge of our Lord Jesus Christ! To lessen, if not destroy, that love, joy, peace, -- that long-suffering, gentleness, goodness, -- that fidelity, meekness, temperance, -- which our Lord works by his loving Spirit in them that believe, and wherein the very essence of religion consists.

To affect these ends, he is continually laboring, with all his skill and power, to infuse evil thoughts of every kind into the hearts of men. And certainly it is as easy for a spirit to speak to our heart, as for a man to speak to our ears. But sometimes it is exceeding difficult to distinguish these from our thoughts; those, which he injects so exactly resembling those, which naturally arise in our minds. Sometimes, indeed, we may distinguish one from the other by this circumstance: -- The thoughts that naturally arise in our minds are generally, if not always, occasioned by, or at least connected with, some inward or outward circumstance that went before. But those that are beyond nature suggested frequently have no relation to or connection (at least, none that we can discern) with anything that proceeded. On the contrary, they shoot in, as it were, across, and thereby show that they are of a different growth.

He likewise labors to awaken evil passions or tempers in our souls. He endeavors to inspire those passions and tempers that are directly opposite to "the fruit of the Spirit." He strives to instill unbelief, atheism, ill-will, bitterness, hatred, malice, envy, -- opposite to faith and love; fear, sorrow, anxiety, worldly care, -- opposite to peace and joy; impatience, ill-nature, anger, resentment, -- opposite to long-suffering, gentleness, meekness; fraud, guile, dissimulation, -- contrary to fidelity; love of the world, inordinate affection, foolish desires, -- opposite to the love of God. One sort of evil desires he may probably raise or inflame by touching the springs of this animal machine. Endeavoring us, using the body, to disturb or sully the soul.

In general, we may observe that nothing good is done, or spoken, or thought, by any man, without the assistance of God, working together in and with those that believe in him; so there is no evil done, or spoken, or thought, without the assistance of the devil, "who worked with energy," with strong, though secret power, "in the children of unbelief." Consequently he "entered into Judas," and confirmed him in the design of betraying his Master; therefore he "put it into the heart" of Ananias and Sapphira "to lie unto the Holy Ghost;" and, in like manner, he has a share in all the actions and words and designs of evil men. As the children of God "are workers together with God," in every good thought, or word, or action; so the children of the devil are workers together with him in every evil thought, or word, or work. So that as all good temperaments, and remotely all good words and actions, are the fruit of the good Spirit; in like manner, all evil tempers, with all the words and works that spring from them, are the fruit of the evil spirit: Insomuch that all the "works of the flesh," of our evil nature, are likewise the "works of the devil."

On this account, because he is continually inciting men to evil, he is emphatically called, "the tempter." Neither is it only concerning his children that he is engaged: He is continually tempting the children of God also, and those that are laboring so to be. A constant watch he keeps; he eyes them night and day; he never slumbers, never sleeps, lest he should lose his prey.

Indeed, the holiest of men, as long as they remain upon earth, are not exempt from his temptations. They cannot expect it; seeing "it is enough for the disciple to be as his Master:" And we know he was tempted to do evil until he said, "Father, into thy hands I commend my spirit."

For such is the malice of the wicked one, that he will torment whom he cannot destroy. If he cannot entice men to sin, he will, so far as he is permitted, put them to pain. There is no doubt but he is the occasion, directly or indirectly, of many of the pains of humanity, which those who can no otherwise account for them lightly pass over as nervous. And innumerable accidents, as they are called, are undoubtedly owing to his agency; such as the unaccountable fright or falling of horses; the overturning of carriages; the breaking or dislocating of bones; the hurt done by the falling or burning of houses, -- by storms of wind, snow, rain, or hail, -- by lightning or earthquakes. But to all these, and a thousand more, this subtle spirit can give the appearance of accidents, to cause doubt for the sufferers, if they knew the real agent, they would call out for help to one that is stronger than him.

There is little reason to doubt but many diseases likewise, both of the acute and chronic kind, are either occasioned or increased by diabolical agency; particularly those that begin in an instant, without any discernible cause; as well as those that continue, and perhaps gradually increase, in spite of all the power of medicine. Here, indeed, "vain men" that "would be wise" again call in the nerves to their assistance. But is not this explaining ignotum per ignotius? {Latin meaning: the action of offering an explanation that is harder to understand than the thing it is meant to explain} "a thing unknown by what is more unknown?" For what do we know of the nerves themselves? Not even whether they are solid or hollow!

Many years ago I was asking an experienced physician, and one particularly eminent for curing lunacy, "Sir, have you not seen reason to believe that some lunatics are really demoniacs?" He answered, "Sir, I have been often inclined to think that most lunatics are demoniacs. Neither is there any weight in that objection, that they are frequently cured by medicine: For so might any other disease occasioned by an evil spirit, if God did not suffer him to repeat the stroke by which that disease is occasioned."

This thought opens to us a wider scene. Who can tell how many of those diseases which we impute altogether to natural causes may be really beyond what is normal or natural? What disorder is there in the human frame that an evil angel may not inflict? Cannot he smite us, as he did Job, and that in a moment, with boils from the crown of the head to the sole? Cannot he with equal ease inflict any other, either external or internal malady? Could not he in a moment, by divine permission, cast the strongest man down to the ground, and make him "wallow, foaming," with all the symptoms either of epilepsy or apoplexy? In like manner, it is easy for him to smite any one man, or everyone in a city or nation, with malignant fever, or with the plague itself so that vain would be the help of man.

But that evil blinds the eyes of the wise, one would imagine so intelligent a being would not stoop so low, as it seems the devil sometimes does, to torment the poor children of men! For to him we may reasonably impute many little inconveniences that we suffer. "I believe" (said that excellent man, the Marquis de Renty, when the bench on which he sat snapped in sunder without any visible cause) "that Satan had a hand in it, making me fall without any luck." I know no whether he may not have a hand in that unaccountable horror with which many have been seized in the dead of night, even to such a degree that all their bones have shook. Perhaps he has a hand also in those terrifying dreams that many have, even while they are in perfect health.

It may be observed, in all these instances, we usually say, "The devil;" as if there was one only; because these spirits, innumerable as they are, do all act in concert; and because we know not whether one or more are concerned in this or that work of darkness.

It remains only to draw a few plain inferences from the doctrine that has been presented.

First, as a natural preservative against all the rage, the power, and subtlety of your great adversary, put on the protection, "the whole armor of God," universal holiness. See that "the mind be in you which was also in Christ Jesus," and that you "walk as Christ also walked;" that you have a "conscience void of offense toward God and men." So shall ye be "able to withstand" all the force and all the stratagems of the enemy: So you will be able to "withstand in the evil day," in the day of severe temptation, and "having done all to stand, to remain in the posture of victory and triumph.

Second, to his "fiery darts," -- his evil suggestions of every kind, blasphemous or unclean, though numberless as the stars of heaven, --oppose "the shield of faith." A consciousness of the love of Christ, Jesus will effectually quench them all. Jesus has died for you! What can your faith withstand? Believe; hold fast to your shield and who shall pluck you from his hand?

Third, if he injects doubts whether you are a child of God, or you fear that you will not endure to the end; "take to you for a helmet the hope of salvation." Hold fast to that hopeful Scripture, "Blessed be the God and Father of our

Lord Jesus Christ, who, according to his abundant mercy, has begotten us again unto a living hope of an inheritance incorruptible, undefiled, and that does not fade away." You will never be overthrown; your adversary will never stagger you if you "hold fast the beginning of" this "confidence steadfast unto the end."

Forth, whenever the "roaring lion, walking about and seeking whom he may devour," assaults you with all his malice, and rage, and strength, "resist" him, "stand fast in the faith." Then is the time, having cried to the Strong for strength, to "stir up the gift of God that is in you;" to summon all your faith, and hope, and love; to turn the attack in the name of the Lord, and in the power of his might; and "he will" soon "flee from you."

Fifth, "there is no temptation," says one, "greater than the being without temptation." Therefore, when this is the case, when Satan seems to be withdrawn, then beware lest he hurt you more as a crooked serpent than he could do as a roaring lion. Then take care you are not lulled into a pleasing slumber; lest he should beguile you as he did Eve, even in innocence, and insensibly draw you from your simplicity toward Christ, from seeking all your happiness in Him.

Lastly. If he "transformed himself into an angel of light," then are you in the greatest danger of all. Then have you need to beware, or you also will fall, where many mightier than you have been slain; therefore you have you the greatest need to "watch and pray, that you enter not into temptation."

And if you continue so to do, the God whom you love and serve will deliver you. "The anointing of the Holy One shall abide with you, and teach you of all things." Your eye will pierce through snares, you shall "know what that holy, and acceptable and perfect will of God is," and shall hold on your way, until you "grow up in all things into him that is our Head, even Christ Jesus."

After reading these two sermons, I wonder if the reason we do not sense the supernatural war being raged around us is because we are not observant. We need to make time to be still and reflect theologically about our day, week, month, and life. God is at work whether we realize it or not.

Have you ever had a Divine Interruption to do God's bidding in someone's life that you were not expecting?

Have you ever had one of your days interrupted with a Divine encounter with another person, a song, a beautiful sunset, uncontrolled laughter brought about by Divine joy?

Have you had a thought in your mind that you were about to complete with sinful bad behavior all of a sudden be interrupted and fall apart by circumstances you did not understand?

How has God been made real in your life today?

What was good about your day and what was not good and was there a story behind the story that dealt with spiritual warfare that may have played a role in the outcome of your day?

As you continue to think, can you see where sin, grace, and hope entered your life in the actions and circumstances around you?

Is God putting a scripture on your heart as you read and reflect?

Reflect on the struggles…where was the love, justice, and peace, and who had the power in this skirmish today?

When Lisa and I were newlyweds, we were driving to Arlington, Texas from the Piney Woods of East Texas to visit my parents and along the way we had an encounter that, if we did not have a Divine intervention, we would not be alive today to tell the story. We were stopped in my little S-10 Chevy pickup under the I-30 overpass waiting to turn under the bypass and to get onto I-30. While we were sitting there, a man bumped me hard with his car. A voice in my head screamed stay in the car! As I looked at the car behind me in the rearview mirror, I saw the man back up and run his car into me again this time twice as hard to the point it jolted my little truck forward. Again the voice screamed in my head: "Get out of there now!" I heard this voice at the same time my eyes were focused on the man's face. I do not exactly know how to describe what I saw; I just sensed evil, and I saw that crazed evil look in the man's face. Whether it was real or supernatural, I don't know, I just ran the red light and sped out of there as fast as I could. When I got to my parents' house, I looked at my truck and amazingly there was no damage! I was expecting my bumper to be smashed and dented. I enjoyed my family for the rest of the day and didn't think anything more about the incident since there was no damage to my truck. That night when my family was watching the news, I saw the man and the car once again on television. He made the news because he had been driving around hitting people's vehicles with his car and when they got out to look at the damage he killed them and stole their money. Needless to say, I had a lot of theological reflection to do that night!

At my church in Livingston, Texas, I had a Perkins School of Theology student interning with me for ten months. Doretta Fortenberry was an incredible intern who was going to be an Army Chaplain upon graduation and after two years under appointment in a church. I was preaching on the "blood atonement" one Sunday and a smell in the sanctuary was so bad I thought I was going to vomit. It smelled like a dead body rotting right next to me. My church in Livingston had a lot of elderly people in it and I thought someone had died and was looking out at the people in the congregation to see who it was. I knew I would figure it out when we announced the closing hymn, and they didn't stand up, and I was preparing myself mentally for that to happen along with all the ministry fallout it would bring to have someone die in the sanctuary. After the service, everyone filed out after the benediction and Doretta and I started to look for where that pungent smell was coming from since everyone left alive. We looked under the pews, we looked in the Central Air Conditioning ducts and went up into the attic that housed the units to see if there was a dead opossum or raccoon that died in the duct work. We even looked for rats, cats, and anything that would be dead and allow that rotting smell to come into the sanctuary. We then went outside and looked on the grounds to see if a coyote killed a calf, cow, or horse. We looked in the trash bin to see if someone dumped a road kill animal or human in the trash.

We both let it go and decided we would bring up this horrific problem to the staff in the morning to see if we could find a fix before the next Sunday. When Doretta and I started talking about the dead smell, everyone looked at us like we were on drugs. We were the only two who smelled it. Even the church staff who was in the choir loft Sunday didn't smell a thing! I asked about those sitting in the sanctuary, and again they smelled nothing at all.

One of the things I do as an intern pastor is work on the intern's ability to think things through theologically. So I am going to give you the assignment I gave her and I am curious as to what your answers are going to be!

What do you want to get out of this session/discussion today?

What was happening in this ministry situation?

How did this situation make you feel and how are you dealing with your feelings?

What was the social dynamic concerning love, justice, and power?

Where did you see sin, grace, God, and did any Scriptures come to mind to help you deal with this situation?

What questions does this raise for you personally?

What are you going to do next after this experience?

Did you work out what needed to be worked out?

Needless to say, we had a long supervisory session that day! What we eventually came up with was that since we had both worked hard on this particular worship service that dealt with the blood atonement of Jesus, invited people to accept God's sacrifice for our sins, and to commit to living lives worthy of that sacrifice, that the smell came about because demonic strongholds were being broken. People were accepting the need to be "washed in the blood" and all the liturgy, scripture readings, hymns, and Holy Communion were steeped in this one concentrated theme. We concluded that a lot of Holy Spirit work was going on in the sanctuary and that God was doing a new thing in many people's lives, and the extraction of the demonic strongholds in people's lives is where the smell originated. My prayer for you is that this little study book helps to make you battle ready by awakening the sleeping warrior within you to engage in the good fight that we are privileged to join!

It is comforting to know how this account is going to end. In Revelation 19, we are informed that when Jesus comes back to Earth at the final Battle of Armageddon, His army of saints and angels will be right behind Him, but we will not even need a weapon because scripture tells us that a two-edged sword comes out of the mouth of Jesus, and that the Antichrist, his evil armies, and evil angels are defeated. That means one word from the lips of Jesus will overcome the evil of this world and the devil's vicious king. Just like in creation when God spoke the world into existence, Jesus will mention one word and end the war. This is the scene that was in Martin Luther's mind when he wrote one of the most famous hymns of our faith, "A Mighty Fortress is our God": "The Prince of Darkness grim, we tremble not for him; his rage we can endure, for lo, his doom is sure, one little word shall fell him." The day of reckoning is coming, and all things will be made right!

Listen to Paul's words of encouragement to the Philippians who, like us today, were living in a multi-cultural world with many gods and forms of worship. Hear Paul's encouragement in Philippians 2:5-13. "Your attitude should be the same as that of Christ Jesus: Who, being in very nature God, did not consider equality with God something to be grasped, but made himself nothing, taking the very nature of a servant, being made in human likeness. And being found in appearance as a man, he humbled himself and became obedient to death—even death on a cross! Therefore God exalted him to the highest place and gave him the name that is above every name, that at the name of Jesus every knee should bow, in heaven and on earth and under the earth, and every tongue confess that Jesus Christ is Lord, to the glory of God the Father."

"Therefore, my dear friends, as you have always obeyed—not only in my presence, but now much more in my absence—continue to work out your salvation with fear and trembling, for it is God who works in you to will and to act according to his good purpose." (NIV)

Pray the following prayers for protection against demonic oppression.

I affirm that God has seated me with Christ Jesus in the heavenly realms far above all principalities and supernatural powers of darkness.

I now command all wicked spirits to cease their work and be bound in the presence of the Lord Jesus Christ. I also bind all replacer wicked spirits assigned to rebuild evicted strongholds. They may not do that!

I forbid any transference of spirits, dividing, restructuring, or multiplying of wicked spirits working against me, in the name of Jesus.[14]

All powers of darkness having assignment against me must hear and obey God, who is their Creator and Conqueror. Lord Jesus Christ, I ask You to tell all of these powers of darkness assigned to rule over me where they must go. Confine them where they can never trouble me again. I yield fully to all of the purposes You have in this battle I have been facing. In Your great name I pray. Amen.[15]

9

CONCERNING MENTAL ILLNESS, NATURAL DISASTERS, ACCIDENTS AND DISEASES

"The real problem is not why some pious, humble, believing people suffer, but why some do not." --C. S. Lewis

When we study the life of John Wesley, we come to understand that he was living in the midst of hand-to-hand combat with Satan and his/her minions. My experience is whenever the Holy Spirit is manifested in a believer; the evil one seeks to destroy the move of God. So if Wesley is preaching to the coal miners and they are moved by the expression of salvation, to the point that there is a physical manifestation of tears streaming through coal-ashen faces, then you know without a doubt that the Holy Spirit has moved them to the point of conviction, forgiveness, and acceptance of God's grace through the blood of Jesus Christ. This becomes something that Satan is not going to want to happen. One of the stories that John Wesley passes down to us was his experience of such an attack. There is one episode where he was preaching outdoors in the middle of a town square and a man who had it out for Wesley started a stampede of cattle through the middle of the city to destroy him. Miraculously, the stampede divided and went around Wesley and the crowd to whom he was preaching. Another time was at the very beginning of his life when John was nearly killed by a raging fire that destroyed his childhood home. There are even academics that have suggested that some angry members of John's father's church started the fire to get rid of the pastor and his family. (All of these are stories taken from my personal class notes obtained during my seminary years in Dr. Richard Heitzenrater's class.). It is in the midst of all this warring and chaos that John Wesley makes these reflections.

Listen to what Wesley conveys in his sermon on Evil Angels:

> "And innumerable accidents, as they are called, are undoubtedly owing to his agency; such as the unaccountable fright or falling of horses; the overturning of carriages; the breaking or dislocating of bones; the hurt done by the falling or burning of houses, -- by storms of wind, snow, rain, or hail, -- by lightning or earthquakes. But to all these, and a thousand more, this subtle spirit can give the appearance of accidents, to cause doubt for the sufferers, if they knew the real agent, they would call out for help to one that is stronger than him." [16]

He is implying that demons try to literally trip you up to keep you from doing the work God would have you do. So when John fell down some steps, or his horse was spooked, or there was a carriage accident, it was the act of demons trying to thwart his ability to make it to the next town to preach the Good News, and he could recognize it for what it was.

This also raises the questions: If I am never attacked, does that mean I am not engaged in doing God's Kingdom work? If you are not being attacked, then are you not doing anything but being self-indulgent instead of sacrificing to do God's work that God has called you to do? The simple answer to both is no. However, it is important to note that when you seek out God's call in your life, you put your life and your very well being at risk. To ignore your calling is to live a life of mediocrity and that keeps you off Satan's radar to be targeted. One only need to study the book of Job to see that he was a godly man and never once gave in to the temptation of cursing God and giving up on God's providence.

When Wesley talks about natural disasters, it is my belief that these things were simply a major inconvenience to him being able to make it to a meeting, or a field-preaching event. We also have to take in account that before the fall of humanity none of this natural bad behavior was happening. It is a result of evil entering into the world through the original sin event.

I do not believe that God sends natural disasters to punish people. Jesus made this abundantly clear in Luke 13. At a time in history when people (Galileans) were murdered by Pilot while making sacrifices at the temple in Jerusalem, there were eighteen men who died when the tower of Siloam fell on them. Jesus must have sensed the questions going on in the hearts of those he was teaching because he said: "Do you think those Galileans were worse sinners than other people from Galilee? Is this why they suffered? Not at all. And what about the eighteen men who died…were they the worst sinners in Jerusalem? No…" (NLT) So Jesus is saying that God does not reward or punish people because of their behavior but emphasized that we all need to repent and be saved so if a disaster befalls us we will be prepared for our eternal outcome.

In Matthew 5, Jesus points out that God does not show partiality on good and bad people, so you need to be right with God in case circumstances fall your way which destroy you. Look at what Jesus divulges in Matthew 5:45: "In that way, you will be acting as true children of your Father in heaven. For he gives his sunlight on both the evil and the good, and he sends rain on the just and on the unjust, too." (NLT)

Sickness takes an enormous plight on many people and causes severe suffering and pain. Wesley says it is hard to explain why this suffering is allowed to happen. He even alludes that God allows it in some situations to make us stronger Christians. I believe God can use all circumstances in our lives that are bad and redeem them. The scars will always remain, and we may never be the same person again, but we can overcome and become stronger for surviving the disease. I was able to witness this firsthand in my wife's life. She is left with the scars of overcoming breast cancer with a double mastectomy and numerous surgeries. She is a stronger willed person, deeply more spiritual and able to do more ministry than ever before. Did she deserve this? No. Did God send this pestilence on her to try to destroy us? No. Did God allow this to happen? Yes. Did God do a Romans 8:29 on us? "And we know that in all things God works for the good of those who love him, who have been called according to his purpose." (NIV) Absolutely! Is our faith stronger after the event? Yes! Are we more acutely aware of the evil that is around us? Yes! Is sickness a result of the fall of humanity? Yes!

So, needless to say, I have some reservations with John's sermon when he says: "There is little reason to doubt but many diseases likewise, both of the acute and chronic kind, are either occasioned or increased by diabolical agency; particularly those that begin in an instant, without any discernible cause; as well as those that continue, and perhaps gradually increase, in spite of all the power of medicine. Here, indeed 'vain men' that 'would be wise' again call in the nerves to their assistance. But is not this explaining ignotum per ignotius? {Latin meaning: the action of offering an explanation that is harder to understand than the thing it is meant to explain} 'A thing unknown by what is more unknown?' For what do we know of the nerves themselves? Not even whether they are solid or hollow!" [17]

On one thing I do agree with John, we do not understand it, it is hard to explain, and when we do, many times it just makes us more confused. I also agree that sickness is a result of the fall of humanity when sin entered the world. That is why "For now we see only a reflection as in a mirror; then we shall see face to face. Now I know in part; then I shall know fully, even as I am fully known." (I Corinthians 13:12 NIV). We live in an imperfect state of being in an evil-induced world where life seems like one convoluted riddle after another. But the day will come when we will see our Creator face to face and we can put all the fragments of life together and see what God weaved out of our lives. Then we will be able to see the big picture and understand why.

Demon possession is real; it is not a medical or psychological condition that can be fixed solely with medication and counseling. Rather, it is a combination of extracting the demons by revealing to the individual what he/she needs to seek forgiveness for and Christian counseling along with medication when needed. That is not to say that ALL mental illness is demonic but it is to say that demonic possession is a possibility. Wesley and many of his colleagues believed the same way: "Many years ago I was asking an experienced physician, and one particularly eminent for curing lunacy, 'Sir, have you not seen a reason to believe that some lunatics are really demoniacs?' He answered, 'Sir, I have been often inclined to think that most lunatics are demoniacs. Neither is there any weight in that objection, that they are frequently cured by medicine: For so might any other disease occasioned by an evil spirit, if God did not suffer him to repeat the stroke by which that disease is occasioned.'"[18]

Have you had an experience with a demonic oppressed person?

Have you ever experienced a demon possessed person?

Have you had things happen in your life that thwarted what you needed to get done? Was there any demonic activity in these roadblocks?

Have you had an accident that you thought was a result of a demonic attack?

Why do bad things happen to good people?

Look up Psalm 35 and cry out to the Lord for deliverance from your enemies using David's Lament to God as your own. David had people in his life that hated him without any just cause! This is a great model prayer for all that are under oppression and psychological abuse from others.

10

CASE STUDIES

"Normal people tend to do wrong, feel guilty, take responsibility, and atone. But dysfunctional people tend to do wrong, justify what they did, blame others, and disrespect the victim." — Robert E. Baines Jr.

As a pastor, I have witnessed several times in my career, the manifestation of demonic oppression and have been at war, as Paul describes in Ephesians 6, not with flesh and blood but with the principalities of this dark world. They choose to manifest themselves in bringing out the very part of human nature that we despise and reject. Sadly, it has become something that most Pastors experience at least once in their career. Various types of personality disorders can cause people to be influenced by demonic activity (oppressed) that cause harm to the pastor, the church, and thwarts the ability of the church to fulfill its mission. Remember, we are talking about two kingdoms in conflict and you can bet that when you are doing what is right and in the will of God, Satan is going to try his hardest to thwart you being used. This demonic activity also affects workplace violence, mobbing, and bullying. You can often see it manifested in the news in multiple stories of Jihad and hate crimes. In spiritual warfare, it is good to understand the story behind the story. I have interviewed people and will share multiple experiences of my colleagues in ministry. I will also share with you the times that we have personally prayed against an attack and were able to help people be restored with God and peace brought back into their lives. After all, this is the mark of our journeys. Hear their stories. Many of them may appear very familiar to you. Many may seem shocking to you. But all are a reality that is growing and we have a responsibility to help mankind find restoration with God and find forgiveness, freedom from chains and reconciliation with each other and God.

- "In one church, I had a parishioner who was consistently complaining about everyone and everything imaginable. Each Sunday we pass out attendance cards in the pews. One Sunday she marked on the pad that she wished to speak with the pastor. I called her up to make an appointment to go by and visit. She responded with: 'I just checked that spot to see if anyone ever looked at those stupid things.'

"I assured her that I looked every Sunday afternoon, and that is why I was calling and that I would be on my way over for a visit. She said, 'No need; I was just checking to see if you were doing the job you are paid to do!'

"I said I was on my way over now since she checked the box with intent to harm." At the moment I was furious with her and was going to let her know I was doing 'my job' to the best of my ability. I never dreamed that it was to be a Divine moment with an intervention. When I got to her house, I said, '_____, I want you to know that the previous three pastors warned me about you and how mean you were to them and their families. One of them even called me and gave me his condolences when I got this appointment. So I just want you to know I am not going to put up with your shenanigans anymore, and I am going to call you out every time you engage in bad behavior. I just want to warn you now that, if you do it in public, I am going to call you out in public, and it is not going to be pretty because this behavior is stopping with this pastor.'

"She immediately began to break down and cry. Through the next couple of hours, I began to understand why she was so demonically oppressed to want to cause pain to all the people she came into contact with. It was because her dad had an affair with another woman while her mother was dying of cancer. The child that was a result of the affair was born blind because her dad had contracted syphilis. She, in turn, had raised this blind child with much bitterness and disdain and lashed out of people in her pain. Wounded people wound people because they do not seek out forgiveness and healing. They want others to hurt like they hurt. Some of these folks even develop psychosis in such a way that they actually derive pleasure from hurting other people. There is no better target than a rational person to attack because your happiness causes them pain.

"When she forgave her dad and those people that hurt her she became a loving and kind person. She eventually allowed God to heal and transform her, and she became one of the hardest working and most loyal members in the church. I am constantly amazed at the transforming power of Jesus Christ in one's life when they allow him to do a new work in their lives. It is imperative in spiritual warfare that we constantly do our forgiveness work, or we will become like who we do not forgive."

- "One parishioner was so broken that anytime a pastor promoted change, they would begin a letter-writing campaign against the pastor to ensure that the pastor understood they were in charge. The majority of the church members didn't like what this lay person was doing but felt that there was nothing they could do because they didn't want to appear mean and hateful. So the bad behavior was condoned with silence and eventually the good people just left the church because they didn't want to be a part of the chaos."

- "Other parishioners love to work behind the scenes and incite discord by spreading gossip, twisted truth, and half lies to crater any plans if they were not their own personal plans. I have discovered that most of these types of members have a deep seeded pain of rejection and have never really accepted God's grace. Therefore, the control they receive gives them comfort and fills the void of their pain. One member in particular was caught in the Sanctuary yelling at the Associate

Pastor about the 'color of the carpet' and wanted to know 'why she wasn't consulted'. When stopped by the Senior Pastor with the question of 'What does this have to do with the Kingdom of God?,' her response was 'What in the world does that have to do with it!'

"The Senior Pastor's response was, 'Exactly. What color the carpet is has nothing to do with the Kingdom of God. Now stop being a bully and leave.' This same parishioner would show up to every single meeting and take notes and then would throw temper tantrums at the meetings and storm out. During one of this member's bursts of anger, she actually hit the pastor in the back of the head with her notebook and then left the room."

This is what happens when evil is not confronted. And so many times it can be confronted without demonizing the person. However, when the pastor does not confront bad behavior, which is often a form of oppression, then the demonic monster just keeps growing to the point that the church declines for decades. It does not matter where the church is located if the people inside are not free to serve God with joyful obedience.

Unfortunately, so many times these members create so much turmoil that the church gets a horrible reputation of chewing up pastors and spitting them out. Herein lies the problem when a pastor is not free to confront evil. Too many times their supervisors will not allow confrontation because they want to maintain peace at all costs. When there is an ideological difference in leadership, then the pastor's hands are tied and oppression wins. Let's look at a few more case studies.

- "One parishioner was a sweet and beautiful woman on the outside with the appearance of really caring for the youth of the church and wanting to be a part of the ministry team. When this person was good, she was really good. However, once I got to know her better, the reality of her poor broken life began to take shape. During long discussions with this individual, she would share personal things with me that had brought her deep pain, and one of them was un-forgiveness in her heart toward people that had hurt her in her life.

  Un-forgiveness is a deep pain that binds our hearts and allows the enemy to oppress us into believing that nobody understands us and that the only way to make the pain stop is to get even! I hurt for her and wanted her to find wholeness and joy. I knew that she understood God and all that He had to offer her but she hadn't really embraced it yet. I'm not sure any of us really ever understands the full capacity of God's grace. Needless to say, she was desperate for it. I spent hours with this woman. I would go on walks with her to help her exercise, because I knew that her health was an issue and a part of the oppression. She wanted to stop drinking. Wanted to stop her affair with a married man. Wanted to be a better Mom to her children. Wanted to get her life organized so that she could live a full life rather than just living one day at a time by the seat of her pants. She was constantly in financial stress. At one point, I even helped her plan menus and grocery shopped with her on a weekly basis. My husband and I would give her money, help pay her bills, babysit her children. Anything we could do to help her get better. But she never wanted to repent of her bad choices or change. She just kept making excuse after excuse.

"After leaving her children with us for a 'weekend getaway' with her husband to some casinos and not returning for a full week without letting the children know where they were or any phone to reach them by, my husband told me it was time to break off the relationship. Finally, when my husband and I broke her off from our financial giving and emotional support, she began a campaign against us using slander, lies and gossip. She managed to achieve her goal by partnering with another member and we were both rejected from our congregation and were re-located to another church. We were told that we should never have gotten involved and that we made the mistake of trying to help!"

- "One individual shared that he was rooming with a psychic and a fortune-teller and said that he hated his church because the church rejected his gift. This individual felt that this gift was from God and by what authority did we condemn that gift. When told multiple scriptures that supported my argument, he decided to spread gossip and lies about me. None of it was true, however, the damage was already done. And I was told that I could not reprimand this young man because 'we don't believe that evil even exists.'"

- "One parishioner, who was upset with me because I wasn't doing what he told me to, photo shopped pictures of me from the parish website onto a porn web-site, doing unspeakable things to people of both genders as well as barnyard animals. He then sent these photos to my church hierarchy as well as other parishioners."

- "Another parishioner would park his car across the street and discharge his pistol in the direction of my office window as a 'notification' that he was displeased with me. He finally stopped when some parishioners told him that if he killed me we might not get another priest for quite a while; finally somebody else parked in our parking lot to return fire from him if he shot towards me. True story."

- "I will definitely tell you that narcissism, borderline personality disorder, and their clustering in my first church turned me off of full-time church work. I graduated from college with a Degree in Christian Education and Music and my husband was in medical school so I looked for a job exclusively near his school. I got a job with a medium-sized church that had about three hundred people in regular attendance for Sunday worship. It had a lot of multigenerational families (families with two, three or four generations in the same church) although many people had to drive a long way and this was a large metropolitan area.

  "As it turned out, it was very inbred from a social standpoint. The same people were always on the nominating committee and held the important church positions. They just shifted around every year. As time progressed it became apparent that there was infighting particularly around the issue of traditional main line church institutions and theology and the local Seminary theology and their literature, students, etc.

  "There was a woman who had been the children's director just before me. My boss, who was near retirement at the time and very well respected amongst her peers, had to work to get this woman dismissed because she was actively promoting dissension and strife. She conducted a children's church at the same time as Sunday morning worship. She kept this position although the pastor had managed to convince the Staff committee that she needed to go as children's director.

She had been a friend with a lot of people in the church for decades. She is the person that a lot of the church strife revolved around. Her husband contributed, too, but she seemed to be the lightning rod. I was just glad to get a job, and wasn't worldly-wise enough to know that this was a horrible situation for me.

"This woman, along with the people she was allied with, worked hard to trip me up and tried to get me to pick sides. Of course, the issue is that there were no 'sides' --- there was always so much drama, and somebody was always mad at somebody else. The only way to pick a 'side' was to pick a 'person'. Being a psychologist now, I firmly believe this woman had borderline personality disorder. I also believe that dysfunctional people choose to stay in a church because they thrive on the drama that they create. Healthy people will leave that church.

"I also believe that while a multigenerational church (at least one in a metropolitan area) looks like it's family-oriented, it may be that there are a lot of dysfunctional people that thrive on anger and emotional upset. Also, for the most part healthy parents are OK with their grown children and grandchildren moving on and going to church close to their homes. Unhealthy ones are more likely to put emotional pressure on their offspring to stay in the same church."

- "I have a list from my previous church-
  1) Being heckled during the sermon by a member of the congregation.
  2) Being chewed out by a parishioner after Easter, in front of several people, for not preaching an Easter message she liked.

3) A member of the church, was caught by me making photocopies of the Choir's ultimatum to me before Church Council which was an ambush that she had co-led with them demanding that young adults should never be able to touch the soundboard again. The best sound board volunteers were the young adults. Our young adult leader left that meeting crying, and he never came back. To this day, he has no place for the church in his life because of the barbaric behavior of these members.

4) Often times, the person in charge of the soundboard would turn off the soundboard when it was time for me to preach and leave with their friends. People of the choir and congregation would applaud after the special music, and then get up and leave before the sermon. Some would slam the door as they left, but that was more rare. Families with young children and young adults stopped coming after we were run off due to the huge amount of disrespect and conflict.

5) While I was visiting elderly members some members would try to find out who I would visit, and then go visit after me to slander me: "Oh, the pastor came by? Let me tell you about him... he hates old people, and he only wants your money." After these things were said to the members, I went to visit one lady and I saw her grown daughter with her (who I had never met). I introduced myself as her pastor, to which the daughter promptly said, "No you are not, get out of here! Now!" At that point she grabbed me by the arm, dug her claws in, pushed me out the door, and closed the door. I continued to make my pastoral visits to Mrs. X, her husband was there, and

after I asked how she was doing, he asked, "Why do you care? We old people are nothing to you, preacher." He said this in the dining area in front of other visitors and guests. He proceeded to curse me out, and rant about incoherent things. I politely dismissed myself and left. She died soon after. They asked another pastor in town from another church to do her funeral, but they wanted to do the reception at my church. Someone else in the congregation indicated that it would not be appropriate for me to show up. So I didn't.

6) The church's old guard had a history of preventing repairs to the church provided home when they didn't like the pastor. I had heard that, but experienced it first hand. We had a washer machine spigot that broke. One of the church leaders, along with some of his allies, didn't want it fixed. It was more of a 'Oh yeah, we'll handle it. We'll get around to it sometime. It might take a while.' We hired a plumber to get it fixed. The church leader was LIVID at the next meeting. The church leader was outraged that we had gone around them to get a repair done. They didn't care that my wife was soon to give birth, and was running clothes to the next town to do laundry. Even with a fund created to fix the parsonage, there were still control issues and passive aggressiveness with preventing repairs from happening in a timely manner in order to hurt me by hurting my family.

"With all this said, yes, there were totally awful people as a part of the church who ran it, owned it all, and had no spiritual maturity whatsoever. There were also great people who fought for a brighter future for the church with us (and lost, as we did). There were good people with good hearts who stayed silent while the bad people did whatever they wanted. Do I think that church has a future? No. I think many of our churches are like that. Toxic. Closed off to the community. Immature. Ineffective. Failing. Did I make some mistakes and bad decisions? Sure. I should have let some staff go sooner. I wish I had. I was worried it would cause terrible fallout and make the church a miserable place to be pastoring. Sadly, it was anyway, without letting the staff person go, and in the end the individual ended up resigning.

"I am tired of my institutional church panicking about a clergy shortage. We need a clergy shortage. Churches like the one I described need to be told, 'If you keep abusing clergy, we will stop sending them. We're running out.' And they will eventually face closure. If word gets out that churches are folding left and right, because they constantly abused the clergyperson sent to them and were not sent anymore, maybe there will be complete, systematic repentance, down to the core, and we will see vital congregations that way."

This tragedy cycles on and on, and we wonder why the outside world loves Jesus but hates the church. We wonder why clergy leave the ministry in droves every month. When I say leave, I mean that many are done and never darken the doors of a church again. To do so brings up too much pain in their lives. The sad part is it is not uncommon for twenty-eight percent of the average attendance to leave the church when a pastor is forced out by evil intentions. Unfortunately, the bullies and toxic people are in control of some of our churches, and I pray for protection for anyone appointed (employed) there. If a church has a history of running off pastors, refuse to work there or be appointed there. If you attend a church that is abusive to its clergy, then you need to move on to a healthy church. One member, who had joined one of my churches, had recently moved from a congregation that had a history of clergy assassins running off preachers. They said that they were so engrossed in the dysfunction that they forgot what it was like to worship in a healthy church. I also had six people visit a church I was pastoring because they could not run off their pastor. When I greeted them that afternoon, I told them to go back to their old church and work it out. I did not want to receive six potential toxic people in the church that would slowly destroy it.

We need to train churches to identify and spiritually fight this oppressive problem because the demonizing oppression has blinded many people to the truth of what is going on in the church. There are a lot of awesome churches that are doing tremendous Kingdom work. There are also some churches that are so toxic that they are successful in their psychological abuse, mobbing, and bullying that they effectively can run pastors off.

While reflecting on these cases, we find that one parishioner sought out repentance and forgiveness and was transformed. In other cases there are those that receive pleasure in causing pain and harm towards others. In yet other cases, the parishioner would maintain control at all costs and the end justified the means. I am astonished at how toxic people seem to attract other toxic people, and they love to congregate together in a cesspool of demonic oppression. It can be a social group, a Sunday school class, or a group of friends. Bad church DNA begets bad DNA. Spiritual warfare is real, hell is real, and victory over both can also be real through our Savior Jesus Christ. There have been many victories in my ministry that I have seen and witnessed. I am just trying to give you some case studies that show that evil can exist in the church as well as out in the world.

What can you do to expose evil or toxic people in your life?

Do you practice good boundaries?

How can you improve your boundaries and make them safer for you and your family?

How is your "fight or flight" reflex? Are you caught up in a toxic environment and need to leave?

Pray for God to give you wisdom and protection from those who seek to harm you. In Psalm 71 we encounter an older, more mature David, who is reflecting on how God has brought him through his problems in the past and is asking God once again for deliverance from those who ridiculed him for his faith and wished him ruin. David knew what it was like to be mobbed. King Saul when he believed that David was his rival for the kingship became enraged and jealous. David was Saul's armor bearer, and he would often play his harp to calm King Saul's nerves. King Saul throws a spear at David and misses him twice as he plays his harp to soothe his ravaged spirit. Saul's son Jonathan and David become best friends, and Jonathan warns David of his father's plan to murder him. David flees into the wilderness of En Gedi and Saul pursues him. While the king is sleeping in a cave at night in the En Gedi Hills, David sneaks past the guards and goes deep into the cave where the king is sleeping and cuts off a piece of his robe. He shows it to King Saul the next day to prove to him that he did not want to harm the king because he could have easily killed him in his sleep. Years later David's son Absalom tries to overthrow his father. Once again we see David escape to the wilderness beyond the Jordan River towards En Gedi to hide. David has a lot to teach us about praying for deliverance from toxic people who desire to harm us. Read out loud Psalm 71 as your prayer of deliverance.

11

THE DEMONIC PLAGUE OF UNHEALTHY NARCISSISM

"One scary point: People with NPD (Narcissistic Personality Disorder) can be vicious when frustrated. Divorce can regress them further and sometimes domestic violence is possible. Whether you buy into the NPD diagnosis or not, it is dangerous to be in a position of vulnerability with someone who feels justified in hurting you because he or she has lost control. Many women (and some men) can't get their heads around the fact that someone who once loved them can hurt them (or their kids). Get help if you think this is your problem." --Dr. Banschick [19]

"Half the harm that is done in this world is due to people who want to feel important. They don't mean to do harm, but the harm [that they cause] does not interest them. Or they do not see it, or they justify it because they are absorbed in the endless struggle to think well of themselves." -- T. S. Eliot

- 2 Timothy 3: 1-7 "But understand this, that in the last days there will come times of difficulty. For people will be lovers of self, lovers of money, proud, arrogant, abusive, disobedient to their parents, ungrateful, unholy, heartless, unappeasable, slanderous, without self-control, brutal, not loving good, treacherous, reckless, swollen with conceit, lovers of pleasure rather than lovers of God, having the appearance of godliness, but denying its power. Avoid such people. For among them are those who creep into households and capture weak women, burdened with sins and led astray by various passions, always learning and never able to arrive at a knowledge of the truth." (ESV)

Personality disorders are on the rise in the local church. It has become a safe place for them to practice their bad behavior without consequences or recourse. These oppressed folks have an innate ability to prey on the gullible and vulnerable with their cunning plans of destruction to get their way and to stay in control of their kingdom. They will wage an all out assault using others to do the dirty work while they remain hidden behind the scenes pulling all the strings and pushing all the buttons. The end justifies the means and if it means destroying people they will do it without any remorse. They have no empathy and may even enjoy seeing others in pain because of their ability to wield power over others by manipulating others into frenzy against their targeted victim. This is the ultimate oppression of demonic Narcissism Personality Disorder. These folks are emotional con artists. They try to manipulate and control you by controlling how others see you and do it with the willful intent to destroy you!

The old adage that imitation is the best flattery is true. We see this picture in the fallen one himself; his greatest abatement was to imitate God. You are never more like a rebellious fallen angel than when you are a self-centered narcissist. I am amazed how some people who are demonically oppressed by this element of evil are willing to destroy a church, destroy relationships, even destroy their own homes before they are willing to surrender their control. It is the closest to being a demigod that they can imagine and it becomes an addiction that cannot be interrupted. If anyone seems to be a threat to their addiction and need for constant attention, they will lash out rather than give up their place in their own little kingdom. These folks have the "appearance of godliness" but are weak in its power because they "deny the power of God". They become god-like to many members and appear to be worshiped. Many times this happens because a particular person is gifted in the area of singing, teaching, art, or any other form of a people pleaser.

This is the original sin that we deal with on a daily basis. Remember what happened in Genesis? "...eat from it *(the tree of knowledge)* your eyes will be opened, and you will be like God." (Genesis 3:5 ESV) Satan wanted to be like God to the point he rebelled and started his own evil kingdom where he reigns and rules. Workplace system analysis professionals call these little kingdoms "silos"; where everyone has their domain and will destroy each other to maintain their silo kingdom even to the detriment of their very own well-being. It is a social cancer where they would rather kill the host and win their kingdom than move an inch. You can often see this in church staff relationships, where people get stuck thinking that their area of ministry is the most important one. We forget that we are "one body" yet "many different parts". That original sin has to be tempered with daily confession and regularly conceding our own control.

It can also happen within the different committees of the church. I have seen numerous churches allow one committee to rule the direction of the church and the only thing that church does is what that one committee deems necessary. Eventually, the church begins to fall into a slumber of single mindedness and people with other gifts and talents begin to feel useless. Consider what Paul teaches in 1 Corinthians 12:20-25:

> "But now there are many members, but one body. And the eye cannot say to the hand, 'I have no need of you'; or again the head to the feet, 'I have no need of you.' On the contrary, it is much truer that the members of the body which seem to be weaker are necessary; and those *members* of the body which we deem less honorable, on these we bestow more abundant honor, and our less presentable members become much more presentable, whereas our more presentable members have no need *of it.* But God has *so* composed the body, giving more abundant honor to that *member* which lacked, so that there may be no division in the body, but *that* the members may have the same care for one another." (NIV)

When we forget this truth, then the enemy will capsulate our hearts into believing our own version of who God is. This is how the enemy wins and brings division in the church. As soon as you see this, begin praying for God to reveal truth to you and other members.

I have had several friends whom have tried to remove narcissist staff members that ended in disaster. Typically what happens with these personalities is that they have been in power of their position for a long time. And with that season of service comes a sense of security and entitlement. They begin to lose the focus of why they are on staff. They honestly believe that their gift cannot possibly be replaced by anyone else and that worship without them would never be the same.

Often times, these narcissists are overly sensitive and become offended when asked to change songs or sing in a better key that includes everyone. A typical answer is "people can sing down an octave" and defensively tells others how they have been to seminars that prove that the songs should be sung in keys that the lead singer feels comfortable. They go on to say their favorite line: "I have talked to people, and they are comfortable with my key." Trying to include a narcissist in team worship design can be an event in itself. When asked to look at songs that the pastor thinks might go well with the sermon and the scripture context, the defiant narcissist will reject any thought of singing anything that they do not already know or that can show off their vocal abilities or instrumental abilities.

When my wife landed her first big job out of college, she was brought on board to lead worship, teach Christian Education and lead the Youth department. She remembers the day that her boss, the Senior Pastor, brought in a spiral bound book and a cassette tape, laid it on her desk and said, "I want you to learn these songs. This is what I want our worship to look like."

Now she had never played contemporary music before, it was a new concept in churches (1986) but she knew that it was her job to use all of the knowledge she received from her sacred music degree and figure out this new worship style. Never once did she think to say, "I can't do this, so, no, we won't have this kind of worship!" As a believer, she knew that God was challenging her to learn something new; it would require her to trust in God and lean not on her own understanding. This is where the narcissist fails.

Narcissists also tend to only mentor people that are weaker than they are to make themselves look good. Either as a staff member or a committee leader, they will not work with anyone they cannot control. They will try to disguise their reasons with "spiritual" language but their intent is the same; how can this person make me look good? They also do not like it when their protégé becomes better than they. If this ever happens, they will take advantage of destroying that person without getting their own hands dirty. They will find someone who is of questionable character but has the ability to bring out drama and then will defend this person in public for having their slanderous opinions. They will lie to anyone they need to maintain their position. They will organize Sunday school classes and even give them suggested letter outlines to use to accomplish the mission of destroying anyone that gets in their way. Many times their destructive behavior is driven by envy, malice and jealousy. They will spend every waking moment on the phone, going to meals with people, even calling members that have left the church to make their offenses known and make threats that they will follow through with.

The power of oppressive demonic narcissism can drive people to do the unthinkable! How sad it is to allow Satan so much control in a church to feed one staff person's demonic narcissistic need. So if you want to survive as a pastor, you better feed the beast and stay out of their way because they will destroy you. You cannot fire a narcissistic staff member and survive. There within lies the problem in a lot of churches. Entrenched staff members with Narcissistic Personality Disorders will lay dormant until you question them in any way, and then they go on the attack with all their friends in the church they have made over the years. If parishioners have to choose the pastor or the entrenched staff person they have known for decades, the pastor will lose every time! The parishioners have to live with the staff member, but they do not have to live with the pastor. Why? Because, pastors will come and go in the life of a church, but the staff member stays. The perception generated by misinformation that the staff member miscommunicates to the community of faith trumps the truth every single time!

In my view and opinion, I believe the only way a church can survive this ill-behavior is for every staff person to submit a letter of resignation before the new pastor gets to his or her new appointment. When the pastor comes, he or she can pick who stays or leaves over his/her first year. All staff serves at the discretion of the Senior Pastor. We do it in government, why can't we do it on the local church level? Because, self-gratification becomes the rule of the day in the local church, and most of the narcissist entrenched staff has been rewarded for their bad behavior. Bishops, District Superintendents, and consultants cannot manage the bad behavior of a few members in the congregation or the few narcissistic staff members. They only can control the pastor. Therefore, the mob rules in this scheme of getting rid of the pastor and the Bishop, District Superintendents, and consultants are just pawns in the hands of the toxic clergy assassins.

What are the behaviors of a narcissist?

How do you as a parishioner protect the pastor from other parishioners with personality disorders?

Pray these prayers where appropriate.

Prayers in Time of Need

Almighty God, the Father of mercies and God of all comfort, come to my help and deliver me from this difficulty that besets me. I believe Lord that all trials of life are under Your care and that all things work for the good of those who love You. Take away from me fear, anxiety and distress. Help me to face and endure my difficulty with faith, courage and wisdom. Grant that this trial may bring me closer to You for You are my rock and refuge, my comfort and hope, my delight and joy. I trust in Your love and compassion. Blessed is Your name, Father, Son and Holy Spirit, now and forever. Amen.[20]

O God, our help in time of need, Who are just and merciful, and Who inclines to the supplications of His people. Look down upon me and have mercy on me and deliver me from the trouble that now besets me. Deal with us not according to our iniquities, but according to Your manifold mercies, for we are the works of Your hands, and You know our weaknesses. I pray to you to grant me Your divine helping grace and endow me with patience and strength to endure my hardships with complete submission to Your Will. Only You know our misery and sufferings, and to You, our only hope and refuge, I flee for relief and comfort, trusting in Your infinite love and compassion, that in due time, when

You know best, You will deliver me from this trouble, and turn my distress into comfort. We then shall rejoice in Your mercy, and exalt and praise Your Holy Name, O Father, Son and Holy Spirit, both now and forever and to the ages of ages. Amen[21]

Prayer for Peace

Almighty God and Creator, You are the Father of all people on the earth. Guide, I pray, all the nations and their leaders in the ways of justice and peace. Protect us from the evils of injustice, prejudice, exploitation, conflict and war. Help us to put away mistrust, bitterness, and hatred. Teach us to cease the storing and using of implements of war. Lead us to find peace, respect, and freedom. Unite us in the making and sharing of tools of peace against ignorance, poverty, disease and oppression. Grant that we may grow in harmony and friendship as brothers and sisters created in Your image, to Your honor and praise. Amen.[22]

12

TACTICAL MEANS OF FIGHTING

"He who is devoid of the power to forgive is devoid of the power to love. There is some good in the worst of us and some evil in the best of us. When we discover this, we are less prone to hate our enemies." --Martin Luther King, Jr.

While watching a documentary on WWII when American tanks were fighting with German tanks, a German tank operator states, "We were good, but there was no way we could beat such a massive force of tanks; they outnumbered us, and their tanks were far superior to ours." The first step in fighting is to assess the battlefield and decide if you can win, lose or draw. If there is a high percentage that you will win then there is hope; a draw may cost your health, emotional wellness, self-esteem and spiritual beliefs; and a loss is self-explanatory. You can't fight alone or with just several allies especially if you are fighting an army. This does not say let evil rule the world, but there may be a need to differentiate between a spiritual battle, a battle against you as the scapegoat that may also turn into a spiritual battle or other variables that may be impacting your work environment. According to many articles by Human Resource Specialist, some sources of conflict in the workplace are in the areas of needs, styles, perceptions, goals, pressures, roles, different personal values and values/beliefs about your role at work and expectations that are sometimes unspoken or mistakenly assumed. According to an article by Thom S. Rainer the reason why Pastors leave their churches are:

1. **Discouragement and frustration over critics in the church.** Over thirty times this year pastors have contacted me to let me know they resigned from their church due to weariness over critics.

2. **Discouragement and frustration over the direction of the church.** Most pastors come to a church with an eager vision and great hope. Many pastors leave a church when it becomes obvious to them that the hope will not be realized.

3. **Moral failure.** The two most common moral failures are sexual and financial. In either case safeguards were typically not in place.

4. **Burnout.** The flexibility of a pastor's job can lead to one of two extremes: poor work ethic or workaholism. The latter inevitably leads to burnout.

5. **Forced termination other than moral failure.** Just last night I heard about a pastor who was fired because the church members determined they needed better leadership. That reason is one among many I hear more and more often.

6. **Financial struggles.** A number of churches do not take care of their pastors financially. Most are able to do so. A pastor who has to worry about paying his bills will not be an effective pastor.

7. **Family issues.** Obviously the family issues could be related to any of the reasons noted here. But a number of pastors tell me they resigned simply because the entire church experience and atmosphere were unhealthy for their family.

8. **Departure of joy.** Typically a pastor has great joy when he is called to ministry. That joy often continues during the time of training for ministry and entry into the first church. But a number of pastors for various reasons lose their joy in the real world of local church ministry.[23]

Some organization psychologists elude to the fact that it can be very hard for just one individual or a few to change a dysfunctional organization structure and work dynamic where mobbing and bullying is the norm, accepted and ignored by church leaders or management. This is becoming more the norm in our society not only in the public, government, health industry but also religious organizations. To fight systemic deviant organizational structures one may look at this battle as a guerrilla style of fighting many ongoing short wars that you are not looking to win but to cause the other to either subside, accept you the way you are, or buy you some time to gather resources to leave. Most likely, the latter will be the best option in the majority of cases. Filing a lawsuit, EEO complaint, conflict resolution strategies, asking for an outside consultant or organization psychologist will only work in the short term, and it is my perspective this will only serve as a diversionary strategy to buy you more time but at the expense of your mental health and ability to get another job. If the hierarchy hires a consultant, you had better be looking to leave as soon as possible. I believe it is best to use some strategies I learned suffering from my mobbing and some from many others in various articles about mobbing. Remember this is just to help you survive until you get another job (appointment, church).

1. Never, never, ever, ever get angry or be rude to the mobbers, it ALWAYS plays into their hands.
2. Smile and be nice even though they are not the same; it will confuse them and may diffuse some aggression.
3. If possible, see some responsibility on your part in the creation of this mob. This will help diffuse some inner anger and explain some possible causation factors in order not to trigger any more brutality against you.
4. Try to apologize and explain reasons for some of your behavior and reasons for the way you are or are doing things.
5. If possible, attempt to get some allies to talk with, but for support only, not to gather info or get mercenaries in your fight.
6. Understand all your options and know that not all options will work.
7. Better to leave early than later on. Watch for signs that others are preparing for war. Signs like negative comments about you, being ignored or ridiculed, being blamed for things true and or untrue in a defamatory way, undermining your behavior so that people will not trust or respect you.

8. Ask others in a non-confrontational way if they overheard anyone talk negative about you.

9. Don't stay in denial of your need to move on. Admit to yourself about what may be going on. Don't overlook the masses as just playing with you or messing with you. There are reasons why they are putting you through a forced termination exercise via mobbing style, and you may never find out some of the real reasons.

10. Be aware of little hints from others trying to warn you of the upcoming battle or unresolved conflict. Saying such things as: "Don't do anything I wouldn't do.", "Stay out of trouble.", "Keep your head up.", "You know you would be good at that other job.", "It's hard to fit in sometimes, isn't it?", or "You know you are always the last to know what is going on.", or "You know they were talking about cutting your position in a meeting?", or "So and so doesn't seem to like you very much." When these hints take place, you might want to start looking for another job.

11. Seek out therapy and stress management. Exercise every other day. Practice deep breathing techniques because they work.

12. Try to act like this is not upsetting you and you think it's funny what they are doing. This will only help you in buying some time to get out of there on a good note such as getting their hint to leave and not be wanted. This happens all the time in animal behavior and is not always easy to accept. Not everyone is going to like you or accept you for who you are.

13. Don't be self-entitled and say, "How dare they do this!", "This is wrong and horrible.", "It's the end of world." Don't be a martyr. In today's world, most of the courts will side with management and think your entitlement attitude (although

understandable) is all in vain; that your complaints about the injustices that you experienced are petty and trivial. In reality, you have some, but not a lot of rights, and if you do, you may have to prove it in court which will be on the employers' side. When it comes to the church, it is a lose-lose situation because of separation of Church and State. The courts will throw it back to the church hierarchy to handle the problem and they will just sweep it under the rug because they have no control over parishioners with bad behavior.

14. Be kind to yourself. Try not to take this personal where you feel justice may need to be served (even if it's the case), you have little room to stand on. It is better to get out of there, and then fight or sue them. Wait until you leave and have another job. It is always better to start legal action away from the work environment and after you have constructively discharged or terminated your previous employment where you were mobbed.

15. Depression and anxiety will be predominant warning signs that it is time to leave and to negotiate severance pay and insurance. A fight or flight response will be subconscious during the day and intrusive at night causing hyper arousal, insomnia, and anger. All these symptoms are all the main signs you need to leave as soon as possible, my friend, for your sake, before they fire you, demolish your self-esteem, and try to ruin your life.

16. Go with God, forgive them, but do tell people your story when you are out of the situations as to protect others, normalize feelings others have had in past hostile environments, and be a witness to the injustice that took place in your life.

17. Don't beat yourself up too much about the mistakes you may have made that have caused the mob to force you out. Realize that you are not perfect and make mistakes, misjudgments, are stubborn, careless and defiant at times, and very human.

18. Learn from this mistake so you can minimize it or nip it in the bud when you start your new job by asking enough questions, staying informed, avoiding isolation and other office politics.

19. Be preventative about mobbing; know how it starts by one or several incidents or situations and try to minimize damage control by staying ahead of the game and gather informal and formal networks to give you advice on how you are doing and your effort as a team player.

20. Remember we are all human and will experience many sufferings in this life. But you can still be happy in those losses by being free in yourself and your hope that you have in Jesus Christ and His coming Kingdom.

I do believe that a significant antidote in the Christian life is forgiveness and that this is a great weapon to overcome spiritual oppression. There was a sweet parishioner that I had at one of my churches who owned and operated a flower shop. She had her share of heartaches and pain that life had inflicted upon her. She would often tell me: "Do not give them free rent space in your mind." She lived her life by that adage and would forgive and forget. I believe her ability to forgive not only affected her spiritual life but also her gifts and graces. She made the most beautiful flower arrangements for the church altar every week. And the arrangements for Easter Sunday were the most beautiful works of art in the floral business that I have ever seen.

I have another friend who is a pastor's wife and is also a licensed counselor. Her life motto is: "You will become like those you do not forgive." Both statements are so very true! If you do not forgive, that toxic memory will be in the forefront of your mind and will continue to fester bitterness, hatred, and wrath.

If you do not want to become the miserly person that inflicted the pain in your life then you have to forgive them. To forgive is the way we can strive to be like Christ. Not to forgive is to allow demonic oppression to influence our lives. There is a reason God wants us in the forgiveness business. It is the only way to have a healthy, productive, positive, joyful life.

Let's look at Matthew 18: 21-35.

- "Then Peter came to Jesus and asked, 'Lord, how many times shall I forgive my brother when he sins against me? Up to seven times?'

   "Jesus answered, 'I tell you, not seven times, but seventy-seven times.

   'Therefore, the Kingdom of heaven is like a king who wanted to settle accounts with his servants. As he began the settlement, a man who owed him ten thousand talents was brought to him. Since he was not able to pay, the master ordered that he and his wife and his children and all that he had be sold to repay the debt.

   "The servant fell on his knees before him. 'Be patient with me,' he begged, 'and I will pay back everything.' The servant's master took pity on him, canceled the debt and let him go.

   "But when that servant went out, he found one of his fellow servants who owed him a hundred denarii. He grabbed him and began to choke him. 'Pay back what you owe me!' he demanded.

"His fellow servant fell to his knees and begged him, 'Be patient with me, and I will pay you back.'

"But he refused. Instead, he went off and had the man thrown into prison until he could pay the debt. When the other servants saw what had happened, they were greatly distressed and went and told their master everything that had happened.

"Then the master called the servant in. 'You wicked servant,' he said, 'I canceled all that debt of yours because you begged me to. Shouldn't you have had mercy on your fellow servant just as I had on you?' In anger his master turned him over to the jailers to be tortured until he should pay back all he owed.

"This is how my heavenly Father will treat each of you unless you forgive your brother from your heart." (NIV)

Peter is concerned with Jesus' teaching and wants Jesus to clarify exactly what he is saying. He wants to know the exact number of times he has to forgive someone who has caused him harm. In the temple, a Rabbi would teach that "if a man sins once, twice, or three times, they forgive him: if he sins a fourth time, they do not forgive him"[24]. So Peter thinks he is doing a great job when he offers up seven times. After all, that is three more times to forgive than the going rate and we all know seven as the perfect number. Jesus responds: "Not seven times, but seventy times seven." (Matt. 18:22 RSV) Jesus is not saying specifically four hundred and ninety times but is symbolically saying that we must have unlimited forgiveness. To demonstrate the point he is trying to make he tells a story of an unforgiving man that was forgiven a huge debt. It goes something like this.

The servant is forgiven his huge debt, goes out and meets someone who owes him a small amount of money and grabs him by the throat and demands repayment. He ignores the servant's pleading for more time and throws him into a debtor's prison.

When the servant's friends saw what happened, they were distraught and went to the king. The king was furious and called in the servant that he had forgiven the huge debt and turned him over to the jail that tortures people to see if they have any sources of money that are hidden. He would now be tortured until he got the full amount that was owed to the king.

Jesus gives us a warning that God will deal with us in the same way if we do not forgive others because we, like the first servant, have been forgiven a huge debt.

May God give us the strength to do the hard forgiveness work that has to be done. It is painful to recount the hurt, the injustice, the rejection, the pain, and the betrayal, but we must follow the example of Christ and say: "Forgive them for they do not know what they are doing." It takes spiritual work to move through all the emotions of anger, fear, low self-esteem, doubting yourself, and the desire to find a way for retribution. That is why we must "work out our salvation with fear and trembling" because we have to forgive to be forgiven.

Is there anyone you need to forgive toward whom you are harboring bitterness in your life?

What is the difference between the two servants' debts?

How would you feel if you saw your friend thrown in jail for not paying a $20.00 debt knowing that the person who threw him in jail had $10,000,000 in debt forgiven?

How does knowing you are forgiven and washed clean by the blood of Jesus affect your ability to forgive others that have wronged you?

Pray:

> Lord Jesus Christ, in Your great mercy You prayed for the forgiveness of those who crucified You, and You taught us to love our enemies and to pray for those who persecute us. Lord, I pray that You forgive those who treat me unjustly and speak out against me and that You bless them and guide them according to Your will. Take away any bitterness I may have in my heart against them. Lord, may Your forgiveness, goodness and love be revealed in all of us, to Your praise and glory. Amen. [25]

13

HOW TO FIGHT

Over the years, I have learned to ask for guidance and hope from the Holy Spirit to know how to fight fair, firmly and with love. In this chapter, I would like to share what I've learned with you and hope that they help you as they have helped me throughout the years.

- Know you are an objective of people that desire to do you harm.

- Pray in Jesus' name.

- Pray often.

- Pray over your family members, church, pastor, retreats and worship services.

- Rebuke evil in Jesus' name.

- Know God's promises for you. Read and keep a book of God's promises with you.

- Remember, you are not a worthless person, but a person of worth to God...you are a child of the King.

- There is a time to fight and a time for flight. Sometime in life you just have to knock the dirt off your shoes and move on. Like Jesus told his disciples in Matthew 10:14 "If anyone will not welcome you or listen to your words, leave that home or town and shake the dust off your feet."(NIV)

- When you go through pain and suffering there usually is a blessing on the other side that you would not have received without going through that demonic attack. So hold on fast to the promise found in I Peter 5:10: "And the God of all grace, who called you to his eternal glory in Christ, after you have suffered a little while, will himself restore you and make you strong, firm and steadfast."(NIV) I also recommend this scripture from Joel 2:25-26: "I will restore to you the years that the swarming locust has eaten, the hopper, the destroyer, and the cutter, my great army, which I sent among you. You shall eat in plenty and be satisfied, and praise the name of the Lord your God, who has dealt wondrously with you. And my people shall never again be put to shame." (ESV)

- Remember when you are attacked you now can identify with Jesus in a very intimate way that makes that distant heaven a home in your heart because you have been through your very own personal lent.

- Know that this too shall pass, and there is peace on the other side of the storm.
- Develop friendships in the church with people that can be your armor barrier like Jonathan was a friend to David and constantly watched his back. Find people that feel called to be your friend and are willing to stand in the gap and protect and pray for you.
- Do not let toxic people steal your joy.
- Pray for the attackers to be convicted by the Holy Spirit for their bad behavior. While praying rebuke them in the name of Jesus and pray God would lift His protection from him/her until they repent.
- Confront them when possible and point out to him/her their bad behavior.
- If people threaten to leave or resign, do not talk them out of it! Let them go! There is such a thing as Holy Subtractions! When they leave, the whole church will be relieved.
- STAND FIRM 1 Corinthians 16:13: "Be on your guard; stand firm in the faith; be courageous; be strong." (NIV)
- DO NOT LET YOUR PAIN DICTATE YOUR FUTURE.

Another example of having to be battle ready is in knowing how to deal with inappropriate disruptions that take place in committee meetings that are intended to cause harm to a church or individuals. There are tactics that can be used for good or evil, tactics that come from the Office of Strategic Services' Simple Sabotage Field Manual. The OSS was the forerunner to the Central Intelligence Agency (CIA) because it was so successful. During WWII, the United

States government, to wreak havoc by disrupting and sabotaging the Nazis operations and those that sympathized with them, formed this organization. This declassified document is found in section 11.

I have experienced this unconventional warfare before in meetings at the church. I am sure you have experienced a few meetings yourself that have been hijacked by a toxic person.

(11) General Interference with Organizations and Production

(a) Organizations and Conferences

   (1) Insist on doing everything through "channels." Never permit short cuts to be taken in order to expedite decisions.

   (2) Make "speeches." Talk as frequently as possible and at great length. Illustrate your "points" by long anecdotes and accounts of personal experiences. Never hesitate to make a few appropriate "patriotic" comments.

   (3) When possible, refer all matters to committees, for "further study and consideration." Attempt to make the committees as large as possible - never less than five.

   (4) Bring up irrelevant issues as frequently as possible.

   (5) Haggle over precise wordings of communications, minutes, and resolutions.

   (6) Refer back to matters decided upon at the last meeting and attempt to reopen the question of the advisability of that decision.

   (7) Advocate "caution." Be "reasonable" and urge your fellow-conferees to be "reasonable" and avoid haste, which might result in embarrassments or difficulties later on.

   (8) Be worried about the propriety of any decision--raise the question of whether such action as is contemplated lies

within the jurisdiction of the group or whether it might conflict with the policy of some higher echelon.[26]

How do we deal with an individual that wants his/her agenda to take place and dominates the committee meeting and tries to sabotage any attempts to make progress? Here are some pointers that I have found successful in my career.

1. Keep everyone on the task at hand. Say to the toxic person: "Thank you, we have heard your point of view." and then redirect the discussion to someone who has not spoken yet. "Mary, what do you think?" Make sure you get everyone's opinion by calling them out and keeping the toxic person in his place.

2. Avoid deferring the matter to another committee. Let everyone know that the goal of the meeting is to resolve the issue at hand. If the toxic person tries to derail the project, make sure the committee knows that the further the distance between the vision and implementation of the vision, the less likely it is going to happen.

3. If people in the meeting seem to be tired and agitated and are willing to let the bully get his/her way…only then, dismiss the meeting or go to another subject.

4. Stay away from conversations that are not productive, instead talk about the positive things that can happen if you pass this idea or resolution.

5. Avoid playing the blame game but refocus the committee on solving the problem without involving personalities.

6. If the toxic person goes on a personal attack, call them out and tell them that their behavior is inappropriate and uncalled

for. If he/she continues, ask them to leave the meeting until he/she cools off. Do not let them throw a temper tantrum in front of the committee…escort them out of the room! Do not let them abuse and bully everyone in the room.

7. Do not let the tail wag the dog! Confront him/her and call them out in order to let others participate equally. Confront the toxic person publicly in the meeting. Do not confront the toxic person one on one in private because the toxic individual will use your words and twist them against you to cause you harm.

8. Do not let an after-the-meeting "meeting" takes place in the parking lot or on the property. If some desire to do so, then go and stand next to them and do not leave until they break it up. Let them know that it is an illegal meeting without the pastor, or if the majority of the committee members have already gone home, they cannot make decisions on the side. If they have a quorum, then they are holding an illegal meeting. Let them know that it is unethical to meet without the whole committee present.

9. Always be at the meeting early, so the toxic person does not stack the committee with his/her poison before the meeting begins.

10. If someone on the committee says something positive that confronts the toxic person then say: "Thanks, _____, what I hear you say is (repeat what he/she said), is that correct?" That way the positive influencer got his/her point heard and recognized and hopefully will redirect the conversation from the toxic hijacker.

11. Cut the toxic person off and refocus on problem solving and do not agree with anything the toxic person says. Do not feed the beast by agreeing with him/her!

Take a few moments to reflect on this list.

Can you put these points into practice? How?

What are other tactics you can add to the list?

When I was serving one of my churches, I had to make a tough decision concerning a low producing employee. A parishioner that took sides with the employee came into my office and berated me for my decision. The individual asked a lot of questions, and I was able to answer them with understandable reasons while being careful to protect the employee. The parishioner threatened to "call me out" and harm me in front of all my colleagues and the Bishop when the Bishop came to visit for a district event. The individual said she was going to round up all her friends and publicly let everyone know what a horrible pastor I was. This was a huge and important event that we worked hard to prepare for. In fact the Bishop, District Superintendents, the Bishop's high-level staff, and all the preachers and lay leaders in the district were in attendance.

I was in the sound booth when the individual and all her friends came to the meeting. I watched them sit at a table at the front of the gym. The gym was set up with round tables that would seat eight people to foster group discussion. I worked the room greeting everyone and making sure everything was perfect for the Bishop's called meeting. When I saw the room was completely ready, I walked over and sat at the table of the antagonist that desired to embarrass and publicly assassinate me in front of my Bishop and peers.

I greeted everyone at the table and sat down. The Bishop stood up and invited me to pray and to tell everyone where the bathrooms were located. I said the prayer, gave instructions, and went back and sat down at the table with the toxic antagonists waiting for the opportunity to implement their agenda to do me harm. While sitting there, I could feel the evil intent and demonic oppression hovering at that table. I prayed to God to shut their mouths like God did for Daniel in the lion's den. I rebuked their evil intentions in Jesus' name and prayed for protection while pleading for the blood of Jesus to cover the room and for the Holy Spirit to anoint the discussions.

Praise God, He answered my prayers, and they did not say a word, and we had a good discussion at our round table. What surprised me was how aggressive and brutal this individual was in wanting to cause me harm. When the meeting was over, they tried to swarm the bishop with ill will but they could not get to the Bishop because others had surrounded her first and the abusers finally left the meeting.

The point of this story is that you have to confront the antagonist. One way you do that is to surround them with good positive people. You also have to be willing to confront them with a friend. I highly recommend having an intervention with them. Bring two others with you and make an appointment to talk to them. If you do not confront them and let them know this is bad behavior then they will not change nor will they know that they are acting out in an inappropriate way.

Clergy cannot win for losing with these toxic folks so there is no foul or no harm in confronting them directly with a witness. Jesus instructs us in scripture to practice this in the church (see Matthew 18:15-17). Unfortunately, most clergy avoid conflict and since these antagonistic people have never been confronted with their wrongdoing, the monster just keeps on growing until they become clergy assassins. That is why you must confront the antagonist in public or with someone else present. If they repent and apologize, then you have made a friend. After all, we are not fighting flesh and blood. To get repentance and restoration is our goal. But if not, then bring two more people with you, and if you still do not have a good response, then you need to ask them to leave the church. If your church polity or rules of governance do not have a procedure that follows this scripture, it needs to be done. If you have a denomination that makes you have a church trial to remove an antagonist that is disrupting the church then the church needs to make sure they are not in any leadership position and you must constantly surround the antagonist with good people that can keep the antagonist in line by continually calling him/ her out on the carpet when he/she acts out in bad behavior.

Continue to lead courageously and surround yourself with positive forward thinking people. Talk with these leaders about strategies to minimize the effects of the antagonist. Remember conflict resolution does not work because these types of folks do not value you but want to destroy you. There is such a thing as "healthy conflict" where everyone can sit down and listen to one another, compromise, reason, see each person's point of view and come up with a consensus to move forward. Antagonists want none of this. They want to win at all cost.

Keep up your guard and be on your best behavior. The antagonist wants to provoke you to anger but whatever you do, do not fight back. Be nice and cordial when you are around them but at the same time do not be passive aggressive. Answer the attack in a conversational tone and tell them you will get back with them if you are not ready or are too tired to give them an answer. Listen to the antagonist and always make eye contact with them, repeat what they said to you back to let them know you understood what they were saying and make sure you document everything! Do not waste your time trying to befriend this person: they will use everything against you. You have to settle in your mind that the "good ol' likeable and loveable you" who exists is who they hate.

Read Ephesians 6: 10-20. Paul tells us to be prepared for battle by equipping ourselves for war. Our conflict with evil is not only physical it is spiritual. So we need to be equipped with spiritual weapons along with concrete tactics to redirect the toxic individuals. We need the belt of truth to dispel the lies against us. The belt was designed to singe up the tunic so it would no longer be free flowing to be battle ready. The breastplate of righteousness is designed to cover our vital organs. We can protect ourselves by living rightly by observing God's laws. The shoes on our feet to make us to be ready to promote the Gospel of peace. Romans had sandals that laced all the way up and over their calf. These were not flip-flops that would lose traction and can easily fall off your feet. These are shoes that were firmly attached to the foot and leg so as to be able to move quickly and maneuver without losing a shoe. We need to be ready to take the good news of the grace of Jesus Christ wherever we go to bring peace to people by knowing they are saved and are also a friend of God. The shield of faith is a defensive weapon that wards off the flaming darts of the evil one. Romans used to dip their arrows in a thick jelly like oil substance and light them on fire and then shoot them at their enemy. It was an early version of napalm in that when it hit someone or something, it would splash the jelly-like tar on everything and cause an instant fire on whatever the tar splattered upon. Satan is going to try to trip us up and splatter his toxic mess all over our lives. The shield of faith reminds us that we are saved by faith through grace. We attest that Jesus is the founder and perfecter of our faith and that we use our faith for protection. We can connect our shield of faith with other Christians' shields of faith and run the enemy over. There is power in groups of Christians because wherever two or more are gathered in Jesus' name, Jesus is there in the midst with them. We need to protect the most vital organ in our body: our brain. We do this by putting on the helmet of salvation. We must be renewed by the transformation of our mind. We need to put good positive scripture, life events in our mind and filter out bad things that are not of God. We need to feed our mind with good teaching and Bible study to protect our mind from false doctrine or doctrine of demons. Our sword of the Spirit is our offensive weapon, and it is the world of God. We must connect our head and our heart with God's word and put it into action. We can strike out anything that does not line up with Scripture because it is our source for reasoning, keeping traditions that help us on our spiritual journey, and allows us to use past experiences as a guide. Scripture is primary to all we do and how we reason God's will for our lives and is a great source to help us defeat the evil schemes of Satan. Lastly, we need to be praying in the spirit and allowing the Holy Spirit to guide and direct us in the battles that we face.

Prayer Against Demonic Influence

Almighty God, Who delivered Your people from the bondage of the adversary, and through Your Son cast down Satan like lightning, deliver me also from every influence of unclean spirits. Command Satan to depart far from me by the power of Your only begotten Son. Rescue me from demonic imaginings and darkness. Fill me with the light of the Holy Spirit that I may be guarded against all snares of crafty demons. Grant that an angel will always go before me and lead me to the path of righteousness all the days of my life, to the honor of Your glorious Name, Father, Son and Holy Spirit, now and forever. Amen.[27]

14

THE TACTICS OF COLLECTIVE EVIL

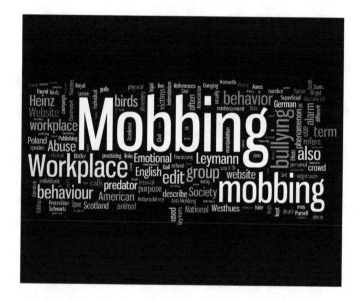

"Research shows that as many as thirty-seven percent of American workers have experienced workplace abuse at some time in their working lives. Mobbing, a form of abuse in which individuals, groups, or organizations target a single person for ridicule, humiliation, and removal from the workplace, can lead to deteriorating physical and mental health, violence, and even suicide." --Overcoming Mobbing by Maureen Duffey and Len Sperry Oxford University Press[28]

"Silence in the face of evil is itself evil: God will not hold us guiltless. Not to speak is to speak. Not to act is to act." --Dietrich Bonheoffer

One of the best ways to fight the schemes of the evil one is to know the tactics of Satan's warfare. Satan's number one target is the church. If he/she can destroy the church and its mission to make disciples, then Satan has decisively won the war. If the evil one can cause people to never darken the doors of a church again or even cause a pastor to leave ministry, then the enemy perceives that as a double victory. So it makes sense that the evil one targets, and sends some of his best assets to destroy a church by mobbing the pastor with collective evil.

Saul Alinsky was a very influential person because he was able to do community organizing to break down some oppressive strongholds of his day. In the 1930's he organized groups of people to fight the horrific working conditions of the Union Stock Yards in Chicago. Later, in the 1950's, he helped organize African Americans who were confined in ghettos. He gave, in his words, the "Have Nots" that were utterly powerless and with no way out of their plight a fighting chance and power to change the oppressive structure that was holding them back. From the outside, these ideals seem to be noble and would achieve great things for humanity. Except that Saul Alinsky used tactics that were written from a dark heart. Saul Alinsky wrote a book called Rules for Radicals in 1971. This book was very influential for the 1960 radicals that were coming of age. He was all for mass riots and stirring up the people for mob power to overthrow the existing establishment. His mob mentality tactics to disrupt and cause harm to those he deems as "Haves" is alarming because not all "haves" are evil. In his book, he proffers: *"What follows is for those who* want to change the world from what it is to what they believe it should be. *The Prince was written by Machiavelli for the Haves on how to hold power. Rules for Radicals is written for the Have-Nots on how to take it away."* [29] Many people over the years have used his mob rules for good and evil. I have personally experienced these rules being used on my own life situation.

One reason I believe Saul's rules can easily be used to promote collective evil is the fact that he dedicated his book Rules for Radicals to the original radical, Lucifer (Satan). In this book this is made very evident by the following statement on the very front dedication page: *"Lest we forget at least an over-the-shoulder acknowledgment to the very first radical: from all our legends, mythology, and history (and who is to know where mythology leaves off and history begins — or which is which), the first radical known to man who rebelled against the establishment and did it so effectively that he at least won his own kingdom — Lucifer."*[30]

"Alinsky's mode of operation would be to find an external antagonist to turn into a common enemy for the community within which he was operating. Often, this enemy would be a local politician or agency that had some involvement with an activity that was causing harm to the community. His goal was to unite a group through conflict with an observable opponent. Once the enemy was established, the community would come together in constant antagonism against it."[31]

I have taken Saul Alinsky's 12 Rules for Radicals and added in parenthesis how a collective evil attack (mobbing) would look in a local church, and it is based upon what I experienced. Comments in italics are mine.

1. "Power is not only what you have, but what the enemy thinks you have." *(I have heard from a lot of people that don't like you.*

People have been saying...) Power is derived from two main sources – money and people. "Have-Nots" must build power from flesh and blood. *(People are going to stop giving to the church and leave or I hear people are going to stop giving and leave. I talked to people who have stopped giving. I have talked to people who have left.)*

2. "Never go outside the expertise of your people." It results in confusion, fear, and retreat. Feeling secure adds to the backbone of anyone. *(Constantly throw unrealistic expectations and scenarios to confuse and bewilder people and knock them off center. Constantly talk about how things were done in the past that were successful but will not work today.)*

3. "Whenever possible, go outside the expertise of the enemy." Look for ways to increase insecurity, anxiety and uncertainty. *(Come up with every conceivable problem the church has and make up problems the church doesn't have then blame it on the pastor. Even though the church has been in decline for years, talk like it just now started with the present pastor. Talk about people who have left... especially those that left before the present pastor got here and blame him/her for them not coming back.)*

4. "Make the enemy live up to its own book of rules." If the rule is that every letter gets a reply, send 30,000 letters. You can kill them with this because no one can possibly obey all of their own rules. *(Use the church polity/rules against the pastor. If it says discussions are confidential in staff parish relations committee, then tie the pastor's hands and feet because he/she has to hold to that rule but you [the parishioner] do not, so spread any misinformation you can find because perception overrules truth especially if the truth is silenced by their own rules! If the pastor cannot speak, he/she cannot defend or protect him/herself. Barrage the pastor and committee members, district superintendent with endless emails. Keep them up*

until 3:00 in the morning trying to combat the lies and innuendo by answering every email.)

5. "Ridicule is man's most potent weapon." There is no defense. It's irrational. It's infuriating. It also works as a key pressure point to force the enemy into concessions. *(Create an environment of anger and fear by mocking every idea and vision the pastor has as incompetent and stupid. The committees will make concessions to the mob, and it will water the vision down so much it will be ineffective. Target a new ministry that is working and say it is not working and come up with all types of lies and innuendo of everyone working with the new ministry to destroy it.)*

6. "A good tactic is one your people enjoy." They'll keep doing it without urging and come back to do more. They're doing their thing, and will even suggest better ones. *(Keep ragging on the pastor...others will join in because it is easy to blame all your personal, community, world, and the church problems on the pastor. You have to live with your friends, but you do not have to live with the pastor because pastors come and go, but your friends are forever... so go ahead crucify, crucify, crucify, and bring a friend to help you. Being a clergy assassin is such a fun blood sport so bring your friends along so they too can enjoy a good beating).*

7. "A tactic that drags on too long becomes a drag." Don't become old news. *(Constantly come up with more policies and procedures that don't solve problems but make them worse. Create surveys and new rumors, and then go out and find people you know have left the church because of the pastor and rile them up with more negative information, so the mob does not get bored and stays in a feeding frenzy.)*

8. "Keep the pressure on. Never let up." Keep trying new things to keep the opposition off balance. As the opposition masters

one approach hit them from the flank with something new. *(Do not let up! Keep new batches of emails coming. Send them to everyone you know and get them to write some, too. Keep them coming every week with a new complaint about the sermon or a meeting, use anything you can against the pastor. Tell people about all the people who are in pain because of the pastor and extrapolate, twist, and add meat to the non-problem and make it look like the worst thing that could ever happen in the history of humanity. Be relentless…never let up on the complaints, negativity, and bad behavior.)*

9. "The threat is usually more terrifying than the thing itself." Imagination and ego can dream up many more consequences than any activist. *(Cause the committees of the church exhaustion by having long and frequent meetings to meet the demands of the onslaught of emails. Let the whiners set the agenda; let the tail wag the dog. Find everyone you can with a personality disorder and rile them up and let them do the dirty work of lashing out at the pastor publicly and anyone that supports the pastor. Collateral damage is good. Hit everyone that supports the pastor with emails nonstop for days. Ridicule them and start stirring up bad things about them!)*

10. "If you push a negative hard enough, it will push through and become a positive." Violence from the other side can win the public to your side because the public sympathizes with the underdog. *(Make the people that support the pastor mad, make the pastor angry, catch him/her when they are tired and vulnerable and use anything you can that the pastor said in an email or in a meeting against him/her and target all those that support the pastor. If a supporter says something negative use it to your best advantage and say: "If they feel that way it must be the pastor's influence on that person." Try to make everyone that supports the pastor so miserable that they*

choose to step down from leadership in exhaustion. If they leave the church, that is not a problem, that is another vote they don't get.)

11. "The price of a successful attack is a constructive alternative." Never let the enemy score points because you're caught without a solution to the problem. *(Always present your agenda to fix the problem and disagree with the solution the committee came up with. Bog the meeting down with lots of useless solutions to sabotage what you do not want to happen in the church)*

12. "Pick the target, freeze it, personalize it, and polarize it." Cut off the support network and isolate the target from sympathy. Go after people and not institutions; people hurt faster than institutions. *(Abuse the pastor, abuse the spouse, target his/her children and make him/her miserable. Cut him/her off from all of his/her friends, make the pastor work eighty hour weeks just trying to stop the flow of anonymous mail and emails that are full of vindictive, cruel, and toxic complaints. Make the pastor have a heart attack, a mental breakdown, commit suicide... who cares if the end justifies the means? And most often, the end is that you want the pastor gone so you can maintain control. Criticize twenty-four/seven and continually come up with more criticism, never shut up or give up.)*

According to Len Sperry, some work group dynamics can be influenced by a sense of narcissism and dependency, disruption and hostility. Sometimes when churches are exposed to their statistics of decline and are shown the need to experiment and try new models of ministry, they become hostile. Because they refuse to admit they are not practicing ministry with excellence, nor do they attempt to improve the few things they do well. So the bearer of truth becomes the enemy and must be eliminated. So this became a form of collective evil that comes from the demonic plague of narcissism in the church group dynamics. The only person that likes change is a kid with a dirty diaper. It is a shame most churches do not know they have long ago soiled themselves and need to change their diaper.

"A group of individuals in the workplace typically behave as a unit or as an ingroup because of group cohesiveness and other powerful forces to keep its individual members together and focused on the same goals. When these forces of cohesion fail, the group begins to disintegrate and ceases to be a group. Two of the more powerful of these group-cohesive forces are narcissism and dependency" (Mantell, 1994). In its simplest and most benign form, narcissism is manifested in group pride. As the members feel proud of their group, so the group feels proud of itself. A less benign but universal form of group narcissism is the creation of an enemy; that is, animosity toward an outgroup. A surefire way of cementing group cohesiveness is to ferment the group's hatred of an external enemy. Deficiencies within the ingroup can be easily and painlessly overlooked by focusing attention on the deficiencies of the outgroup."[32]

It is all up to the lay people to protect the clergy person because the clergy person is a powerless sitting duck who has no one watching his/her back. The Bishop and District Superintendent cannot control the mob no matter how hard they try but they can control the pastor. The only way they can protect the pastor from the mob is to move him/her usually to the pastor's detriment because he/she is a must move. If you attend a church that can successfully run off a pastor then those evil influencers are going to need to step down from leadership and leave the church, or you are going to need to find another church. Unfortunately nothing changes and all the good people leave and the clergy assassins are still in charge. They do not care that twenty-eight percent of the church has left and most of those will never attend a church again. They do not care that the church's reputation in town is now ruined. They do not care that they destroyed a pastor's life and career. They do not care about anything because the end justifies the means. Winning and control means everything! They will even brag about their success and say that it was good for the church to go through this ordeal. I even had one of my clergy assassins say that I was the sixth pastor he was able to run off, bragging about the success of removing the pastor and that the church will rebound now. Typically what will happen is that the new pastor comes in and rewards all the bad behavior (not always knowing what has happened before his entrance) of those that are left and then the good people end up getting frustrated and leave the church. In my opinion, this is exactly why the Denominational churches are declining and failing. They have been placed in a situation that has no workable solution to deal with toxic people. After running off a pastor, these toxic folks lay dormant like a functioning drunk and will arise again for destruction with the next pastor that threatens them in any way.

Hiring a consultant many times does not solve the problem of collective evil and mobbing. All the consultant can do is expose some of the bad behavior. It is up to the church to decide if they are going to just sweep it under the rug or confront the bad behavior that has been exposed. The church will not do this because it is too painful to call out those who participated in bad behavior and they are under the delusion that all this will be solved with a new pastor. The institutional leaders (Bishops and District Superintendents) have to hire the consultant to cover their inability to handle the situation properly because they have no power or control of the parishioner's bad behavior which created the mobbing. So basically you hire a professional consultant who has written books about congregational leadership and all is well. He/she interviews people and comes up with a list of solutions that will not work because the church will not act on them. Nothing changes and the cycle of abuse is not broken. Peace at all cost is preferred over justice.

Like a scene from The Walking Dead, the Zombie Apocalypse spreads their sickness by biting other healthy people. So individuals who are usually normal become toxic by being infected by another toxic person. When the toxic poison spreads to the point that the toxic parishioners will not settle, no matter what concessions the pastor makes to rectify the situation, then without help from the hierarchy to tell the toxic parishioners to leave, the pastor has no other choice but to flee for his/her life. The main reason the institution pays a consultant to do what he/she does can be found in this revelation… "If an individual becomes the lightning rod for people's anxiety and cannot extricate him/herself from that position through self-differentiation (or the environment is so perverse that no one can escape from that position), trying to maintain his or her position or presence in the emotional system is unproductive as well as painful."[33]

The institution pays the consultant, and therefore, the institutional leadership can wash their hands of the clergy assassination because now they have an excuse to do so that is beyond their control. Remember the institutional church cannot control toxic parishioners, they can only control the pastor, therefore the pastor is expendable because many times it is the only option.

The church is the easiest place to be attacked and destroyed because it has no defense against toxic people and the pastor is an expendable target. The best way to confront this evil is to know the tactics they employ. If people will rally and call out and rebuke the bad behavior publicly and ask people to leave the church then, healing can take place. If not, the cycle of destruction will not only continue but will attract even more toxic people with personality disorders because obviously they are welcomed. The good people will leave in droves because they know the church is an unhealthy environment and will continue to be a stronghold for destroying people's lives instead of helping people become all God desires them to be.

- "Warn a divisive person once, and then warn him a second time. After that, have nothing to do with him. You may be sure that such a man is warped and sinful; he is self-condemned." (Titus 3:10-11 NIV)

In Titus, chapter 3, the church is told to avoid "evil works" and focus on doing "good deeds." False teachers who were stirring up false controversies and arguments and quarrels besieged Titus' church. There were Christian Jews who were still following all the ceremonial and Levitical laws and were insisting that everyone had to follow the laws to be a good Christian.

The problem was not so much the theology of following the laws but rather the bad behavior of the false teachers in trying to persuade people to their way of thinking. The divisiveness that they were producing in the church was evil. Titus was instructed to warn this divisive person once to stop. If they continue, warn them again. If it happens again have nothing to do with them because he/she "is warped and sinful; he is self-condemned."

The fact is that these contentious folks are tenacious and will not listen, it means that they need to be rejected by Titus and the church.

Does your church have a way to deal with clergy assassins?

Do you have people that are willing to confront those starting divisions in your Church?

Do you have a policy that allows you to remove people from the church that is causing it harm?

If you cannot stop the mobbing of the pastor, are you prepared to give him/her a paid six-month leave of absence to heal and find another church to pastor or to leave the ministry and find another occupation? This should be the responsibility of every church that refuses to do the right, noble, and spiritual thing.

How do Paul's words to Titus express "tough love" and "choices have consequences" when it comes to those individuals that are toxic in a church?

For more help and information I highly recommend the following website www:workplacebullying.org

Prayer for Our Enemies

Lord Jesus Christ, in Your great mercy You prayed for the forgiveness of those who crucified You, and You taught us to love our enemies and to pray for those who persecute us. Lord, I pray that You forgive those who treat me unjustly and speak out against me and that You bless them and guide them according to Your will. Take away any bitterness I may have in my heart against them. Lord, may Your forgiveness, goodness, and love be revealed in all of us, to Your praise and glory. Amen.[34]

15

OVERCOMING THE SPIRITUAL ATTACK

One must recognize that they need to seek out and work on their spiritual and mental healing after going through an onslaught of spiritual attacks by toxic people. After clergy exterminators and toxic people have mobbed you, it plays a toll on your mental and spiritual well-being. The longer you experience traumatic and demeaning psychological and emotional abuse the more time it will take to heal.

This spiritual attack on clergy is becoming an epidemic in the Church. "Twenty-eight percent of clergy have experienced a 'forced termination' by a few people in a church who make the pastor's life so miserable that he/she chooses to find another church or job. Forty-two percent of pastors that experienced forced termination consider leaving the ministry. They have a high burnout rate and no longer enjoy being in ministry."[35]

In another interesting paper, "Clergy Who Experience Trauma as a Result of Forced Termination" by Marcus N. Tanner, Jeffrey N. said the following in the abstract: "Forced termination of clergy is a demeaning and psychologically distressing experience. Clergy who experience a forced termination are subjected to mobbing (psychological harassment) and other activities meant to publicly or privately demean a minister in such a way that they resign their ministry position. In a purposive convenience sample of fifty-five ministers who had been forcibly terminated, participants scored above the known cut-off score for post-traumatic stress disorder (PTSD) and scored high on a measure of burnout and generalized anxiety disorder (GAD)"[36]

People who have not been through a violent mobbing attack will never understand what you are going through or have been through. I highly recommend you spend time with people who have made it through to the other side and seek their advice, companionship, and prayers if you are in the midst of an attack or just got through with one.

I have personally found that it is imperative that you work through your healing with a good Post Traumatic Syndrome Disorder experienced counselor. I was not getting the help I needed until I changed therapists and found one that had experience working with PTSD clients and uses EMDR (Eye Movement Desensitization and Reprocessing) as a treatment method to be able to recover from the trauma of the attack. I would also encourage you not to be afraid of taking some medication such as Zoloft to help with PTSD. You have PTSD, and you must learn to deal with it and overcome it to be spiritually healthy again in order to stay in ministry or any work environment for that matter. What happened to you was you sustained an attack by church terrorists and workplace mobbing. You were assaulted and abused, and this will cause harm to you if you do not deal with the reality that you have a form of PTSD.

One of the symptoms I went through was withdrawal. I did not want to associate with anyone or anything that would remind me of the events that happened at the toxic church. I became easily angered; it was hard to stay focused, and my memory took a while to function properly again. Some of the bad behavior you experienced continues to pop up in your mind, and you recall events that you no longer desire to remember! You have nightmares of people attacking you…either a recalled memory or made up situations in your mind where you are fighting against people that are terrorizing you with negative bad behavior. You have places in your mind that are blocked out because of the trauma, and that is why you need a therapist that uses EMDR therapy to help you recover and work through the attacks.

You will experience a severe hurt in your body, mind, and soul. Any reminders of the event are distressing and stressful. You will experience intense anger towards those who abused you because there were no consequences for the bad behavior. When peace at all cost is more important than justice, it is hard for healing to take place. Depression takes place because your world has forever changed, that which you loved you now avoid, you have lost your credibility because no one understands what you went through, and you have no desire to maintain collegial relationships. Depression is enhanced because of your desire to withdraw and especially for those that have extrovert personalities. I also had a period where I suffered from Attention Deficit Disorder and could not stay focused or concentrate for long periods of time.

You have to deal with processing all the negativity and hypercritical assaults against you. It takes a while to process over assimilation or over accommodation concerning the triggers in your life that you have to live with after the attack, such as "all music directors and praise team leaders are evil and narcissistic", "all parishioners are bad", "all churches are bad", "all the church hierarchy is bad", "all organized religion is bad". Some people will agree with you in part, but not all will agree, and in many cases, very few will agree. But then again, the old saying is true: "It only takes one bad apple to spoil the whole bunch."

You have to learn all over again to differentiate between true feelings of danger and threats from others; it will not all be directed at you, sometimes it is something not to worry about. Not all criticism is an attack; you have to learn all over again about the concept of constructive criticism. You have to acknowledge that your feelings of hyper-vigilance, panic, anxiety, exaggerated startled response can be so overwhelming it clouds your judgment and insight.

Your sleep patterns get chaotic. You either sleep too long, or you wake up too early. You stay up too late or go to bed too early! Zoloft helps with this and all the symptoms I have listed. Do not be afraid of this medication… take it. I avoided it for six weeks because I was afraid of the stigma of being on psychiatric medication and the bad side affects that could have happened. I praise God for modern medication because it worked wonderfully and helped immensely with the healing process.

I greatly appreciate this ancient prayer from the Greek Orthodox Church:

In the Name of the Father and the Son and the Holy Spirit:
O God, be merciful to me a sinner. (3 times)
O Lord our God, forgive all the sins I have committed this day in word, deed and thought, for Thou art good and lovest mankind. Grant me peaceful and undisturbed sleep. Send Thy Guardian Angel to protect and keep me from all harm. For Thou art the Guardian of our souls and bodies, and to Thee do we ascribe glory, to the Father and the Son and the Holy Spirit, now and ever and unto ages of ages. Amen.[37]

So basically you need to develop new coping skills just like a child learns to walk, you need to learn to walk again. You have to learn to walk again! If you cannot afford counseling or medication, I would highly encourage you to use some resources on the Internet. One great resource I found was a military manual on PTSD.

http://www.mirecc.va.gov/docs/visn6/
PTSD_Recovery_Group_Therapist_Manual.pdf
PTSD Recovery Program Therapist Manual

Here is an excerpt from Page 30
Review: Common Reactions to Trauma

RE-EXPERIENCING SYMPTOMS

➢ Intrusive memories, images of trauma, flashbacks.
➢ Nightmares.

- Intense distress when reminded of trauma.
- INCREASED PHYSICAL AROUSAL
- Hyper vigilance.
- Exaggerated startle, jumpiness. Irritability, anger, or rage.
- Sleep problems.
- Poor concentration and attention.
- AVOIDANCE OF TRAUMA REMINDERS
- Efforts to suppress thoughts and feelings about the trauma.
- Avoidance of conversations about the trauma or related topics.
- Avoidance of activities, places, or people that bring up trauma memories.
- NUMBNESS
- Loss of interest and/or decreased participation in important activities.
- Feeling detached from others, isolated.
- Emotional numbness, restricted range of feelings (e.g., can't have loving feelings).
- Loss of sex drive.
- Hopelessness or diminished sense of a future life.

OTHER RELATED PROBLEMS

- Overestimation of danger in the environment. Loss of trust.
- Loss of intimacy/relationship problems. Impatience.
- Over-use of alcohol or drugs.
- Depression.
- Feelings of guilt or shame.
- Feelings of incompetence or inadequacy.

I have read many books on this subject and the best books I have read that have helped me in my healing are with sampling:

"When Sheep Attack" by Dennis R. Maynard. From page 109–110:

> "If Satan wants to hurt the Body of Christ he needs only recruit a handful of resentful people and have them attack the leadership and divide the congregation."

The Six Red Flags from twenty-five case studies are as follows:

1. There are controlling, angry personalities in congregations that find their fulfillment by attacking and destroying clergy.
2. Congregations that have allowed the antagonists to unseat a previous senior pastor will most likely do it again.
3. All but one case indicated that the antagonists were being led by an active or retired member of the clergy team in the parish. Assisting clergy that had made political pastoral alliance in the congregation were the most dangerous.
4. Neighboring clergy and/or the senior pastor's current or previous bishop often assisted the antagonists. This was especially true when theological, or political differences existed between the bishop and the rector.
5. The bishops and denominational authorities in our case studies were ill equipped to deal with conflict led by antagonists.
6. The most successful method of dealing with antagonists is when all the players in the system refuse to allow the antagonists to triangulate and utilize anonymous sources.

'Healing For Pastors and People Following a Sheep Attack' by Dennis R. Maynard. From Page 172:

Healing Begins

- By shaking the dust from your feet and removing yourself from the parish and all that surrounds it.
- Burying all the negative, traumatic and painful memories under a host of new, positive and happy ones.
- Discharging your anger in a positive manner.
- Turning your hurt and pain into acts of love and compassion.
- Living in the present and the future. Leave the past in the past.

"Wounded by God's People" by Anne Graham Lotz:

"Rejection, disapproval, or abuse by God's people can be devastating because if you and I are not careful, we may confuse God's people with God. And God's people don't always act like God's people.

The way you and I handle being rejected and wounded is critical. Our response can lead to healing...or to even more hurt."[38]

"The Ten Commandments of Working in a Hostile Environment" by T.D. Jakes.

From Page 22:

"God strategically sends people into hostile environments that they might bring about the change that He desires. It is an honor to be chosen by God and sent into a hostile environment. I know these situations can be uncomfortable, but when it's all over God will be glorified and the one sent will be blessed! Just focus on this: God is not as interested in your comfort as He is your purpose. Equate it to physical exercise; regardless of the newfangled exercise gadgets that let you "work out" while you sit at the computer, the truth remains: no pain, no gain."

"Overcoming Mobbing: A Recover Guide for Workplace Aggression and Bullying"

From page 17:

"While workplace bullying and workplace mobbing have abusive behavior directed toward targets in common, they have important distinctive features. Workplace bullying involves an individual or a group of people behaving aggressively and abusively toward a victim, but the organization through the exercise of its leadership and authority is not involved as a coparticipant in it. In workplace bullying, the exercise of power and control over another provides the ignition for the aggressive and abusive behavior. In workplace mobbing organizational leadership and other members support and participate in overt or covert actions designed to drive a victim from the workplace and strips the person of dignity, respect, and credibility."

"Clergy Killer Characteristics" by G. Lloyd Rediger[39]

➤ "Destructive" — CKs don't just disagree or criticize, they insist on pain and destruction for their targets. Their tactics include sabotage, subverting noble causes, pushing others to do their dirty work, and causing victims to self-destruct.
➤ "Determined" — CKs don't stop. They may pause, go underground, or change tactics. But they will intimidate, network, and break any rules of decency to accomplish their destruction. They insist that their agenda have priority.

➢ "Deceitful" — CKs manipulate, camouflage, misrepresent and accuse others of their own tactics. Their statements and negotiations are not trustworthy, unless negotiations are based on enforcement powers or their departure.

➢ "Demonic" — CKs are evil or mentally disordered, depending on how you define intentions and behavior which do not yield to patience and love, nor honor human decency. They are attracted to spiritual leaders as symbols and scapegoats for the internal pain and confusion they feel. And since their mental pain and spiritual confusion are unidentified, these foment unusual reactive and destructive motivations.

➢ "Denial" — this fifth D is the typical church and clergy resistance to admitting the reality and destruction of CKs. And this is how we collude in their nefarious purposes.

➢ "Discernment" — this is the prescriptive sixth D. The spiritual gift of discernment is God's gift of grace proffered in an enlightened mind which sees and understands evil, and then allows itself to be empowered to follow God's Holy Spirit in being an agent of exorcism by confronting evil in the form of CKs. This works best, of course, in a community of faith.[40]

"Clergy Killers Guidance for Pastors and Congregations Under Attack" by G. Lloyd Rediger. Survival Skills for Clergy pages 134-135:

1. Believe that it is possible for someone to want to destroy you.
2. Understand that your denomination typically has little power or inclination to save you from CKs.
3. Recognize that the danger signals and patterns of behavior of CKs can be learned (vid. the "Six Ds" above).

4. Be aware that pro action is far better than reaction in dealing with CKs.

5. Accept the fact of evil and mental disorders are in the church.

6. Expect the attacks of CKs to have serious negative effects on your congregation and loved ones. Therefore, your survival skills are important for their protection and should be taught to them as well.

7. Learn that awareness and survival skills need not produce paranoia, nor rob us of the joy of ministry. They simply aid us in functioning in ways appropriate to contemporary reality.[41]

This has become one of my favorite quotes and it comes from the good doctor in his clinical perspective of a Clergy Killer. In my opinion, this quote was spot on for me and hit the target perfectly. On page 10 and 11:

"A clinical, or psychological perspective on clergy killers indicates that they are likely to have personality disorders (antisocial, borderline, paranoid, narcissistic—which will be discussed later). They may be previous or present victims of abuse. They may have inadequate socialization, arrested adolescence, and violent role models in their history. They may have developed a perverse, voyeuristic, and vindictive taste for the suffering of their victims. In more ordinary terminology, clergy killers have learned the power of throwing tantrums to get their way. They know how to distract, confuse, and seduce. They can wound or kill by direct attacks, by inciting others to inflict the wounds, or by inducing victims to self-destruct." [42]

Pastors, like many people in the helping profession are good, innocent and naive about worldly people, evil and the disruptive nature of group dynamics in social and church organizations. Pastors usually have a Master of Divinity degree (like who can Master the Divine) with absolutely no management courses. Many of us have been raised in middle-class Christian homes and, for the most part, have been sheltered from evil, danger, and a worldly existence because we have spent most of our life in Church. Clergy and most people raised in Christian homes are not prepared for the road of rejection, discouragement, shame, betrayal, and despair that is so prevalent in the world but not expected in the local church. I never dreamed I would be so viciously attacked and that people could be so resolute on hurting me that if I didn't leave they would even be willing to kill me. Mobbing was never in my perception about my career or calling as a Pastor. I know I was not adequately prepared to be mobbed by many who I was supposed to help. I usually work with the best and brightest people on earth and have never had any problems. You may even say I lived a charmed life with great success at the churches that I have had the honor of serving. I have had non-constructive complaints and toxic people in my life, but to have the tables turned and to be made out to be the enemy of the local church by a few people who whipped the church into a high anxiety frenzy intent on harming my family and me was a new experience. We pastors and laity must realize that this should not be a shock due to the nature of religion and the spiritual management of the church and its people. The Bible talks about how the Israelites rebelled against Moses and tried to kill him. Throughout history, many other well known spiritual leaders in the Jewish and Christian faith have been killed, imprisoned, crucified, burned, hanged, and decapitated for their stance on certain beliefs in religious, social change. Many were outstanding people that made much-needed change in the church and faced ruin and death for doing so.

Two that come to mind are Wycliffe and John Huss. Wycliffe translated the Latin Vulgate into the common English language and was persecuted his whole life for doing it. All he wanted to do is make God's word available to everyone. The Church hierarchy believed that the only people who could adequately handle the word of God were the priests and that the Bible would be dangerous in the untrained minds of the ordinary folks. They so hated Wycliffe that when he died, they dug his body up and burned his corpse and writings. That is crazy when you think about it. They hated him so much that they even mobbed him while he was in his grave. John Huss was confronting the hierarchy of the Catholic church for some of their unbiblical doctrines. They burned him at the stake even after they told him to leave and promising him safe passage.

So, in reality, mobbing is nothing new historically but it is new to someone who has been sheltered or has grown up in a spiritual home absent of an impoverishment, chaos, and social disruption. Given this dilemma and antithesis of a healthy environment, it is quite understandable why this doesn't always work out well for those being mobbed.

The first step to overcoming the attack is to realize that you will go through the stages of grief. This is very normal for anyone going through a loss, and this is going to be a major one. Also, this may be accompanied with feelings of anxiety, depression, loss of self-esteem and self-worth, negative feelings and beliefs about yourself, the world, church organizations, feelings of guilt, self-blame, emotional numbing, anger, insomnia, avoiding reminders, thoughts, people and places that are symbolic representations of these past situations and events. Panic attacks or intrusive thoughts may also come up in various situations at home or in other social situations that are reminders of the past event. These symptoms will most likely lessen over the course of several years but reoccur if not adequately dealt with in a constructive way.

Outside of therapy, (and there are many good self-help books about anxiety and depression) it may be helpful to look at some mistaken beliefs that some pastors may have after an all-out spiritual attack by toxic people who created a mob to destroy a preacher. Prevalent in most people with depression and anxiety are distorted thinking and mistaken beliefs that are highly irrational and exaggerated due to the disembarking of a forced termination, being fired, or asked to leave their clergy job. Thus having a good perspective on the real value of life is needed and interest in things you enjoy, as well as support, is a good first start in building up a defense against depression and anxiety.

Possible mistaken beliefs that people and clergy members may experience after the traumatic event of all-out spiritual warfare and the mobbing experienced through collective evil are as follows:

1. I will never be happy or accepted by a church board or congregation and if I am not accepted my life is over, and it's the end of the world. Corrective belief: No. It is not the end of the world or career in ministry but maybe just the end in that church setting.

2. I made a mistake, and I am incompetent and stupid with my decision-making process and the ability to foresee and make right decisions in the church environment. Corrective belief: You are not the only one to make a mistake. As a matter of fact, so did David. God judges the heart so don't be so hard on yourself.

3. My value, self-esteem as a person and as a church leader depends on what others think of me. Corrective belief: This is false; I believe it is what God thinks and not the church members. People are very fallible like all of us and will say and

do things that are against your views, beliefs, personality, and family. They do not dictate your self-esteem or self-worth.[43]

Pray this after an attack to help you overcome and start your healing process:

"Almighty and merciful God, I most humbly and heartily thank Your divine majesty for Your loving kindness and tender mercies, that You have heard my humble prayer, and graciously granted me deliverance from my trouble and misery. I pray to you to continue granting Your helping grace, that I may lead a life pleasing to You, that I may continually offer to You a sacrifice of praise and thanksgiving, O Father, Son, and Holy Spirit. Amen."[44]

16

THE BEST IS YET TO COME!

"Oft hope is born when all is forlorn." --J. R. R. Tolkien

I am amazed at how relevant the book of Daniel is and how it speaks to us right where we are in our modern times. I want to end this book by looking at the providential nature of God and place our hope and trust in God. In spite of the evil that seems to be winning in our world today, Daniel, chapter 12 encourages us, in the midst of what seems to be hopeless, that God is in control, and the best is yet to come!

At the beginning of Daniel's prophecies, we had the angel Gabriel talking to Daniel and giving him interpretations but for him to get there, he needed some help from the Archangel Michael. Daniel 10: 10-14

- "A hand touched me and set me trembling on my hands and knees. He said, 'Daniel, you who are highly esteemed, consider carefully the words I am about to speak to you and stand up, for I have now been sent to you.' And when he said this to me, I stood up trembling. Then he continued, "Do not be afraid, Daniel. Since the first day that you set your mind to gain understanding and to humble yourself before your God, your words were heard, and I have come in response to them. But the prince of the Persian kingdom resisted me twenty-one days. Then Michael, one of the chief princes, came to help me because I was detained there with the king of Persia. Now I have come to explain to you what will happen to your people in the future, for the vision concerns a time yet to come." (NIV)

I love how Gabriel needed God to call out the big gun Michael, the warrior angel, to fight and defeat the evil angel that was over Persia. It took twenty-three days for Gabriel to get to Daniel to give him God's prophecy concerning the future. Twenty-three days! So apparently there are evil angels that are over providences. Michael, the protector, is finally going to wrap up all this evil nonsense for good.

When we look through the book of Daniel, we can expect to have tough times. Daniel 12:1 "At that time, Michael, the great prince who protects your people, will arise. There will be a time of distress such has not happened since the beginning of nations until then." (NIV)

You can imagine how Daniel's heart sank along with the rest of the exiled Jews. I am sure they are thinking what you and I are thinking: Are not things supposed to get progressively better?

I love Walt Disney World's longest-running stage show "The Carousel of Progress." In this show, animatronic people give us a history of the progress of an average family throughout 20th century America. They go from a bucket of water to a pump in the kitchen to running water, candles, to gas lights, to electric lights to time-saving appliances from ice boxes, to refrigerators and futuristic appliances yet to come. I love the song that goes along with every time change as the stage rotates before our very eyes with yet another scene of progress. It is a catchy tune: "There is a great big beautiful tomorrow, Shining at the end of every day. There's a great big beautiful tomorrow, And tomorrow's just a dream away."[45]

It truly is amazing when you think about all that humanity has accomplished! However, the book of Daniel shows us, that in spite of all the progress we are making civilization continues to get more and more corrupt. "Then there will be a time of anguish greater than any since nations first came into existence..."(Daniel 12:1b NLT) We do not have to watch the news very long to see that radical Islamic terrorists continue to spread their collective evil in Russia, Israel, Colombia, France, USA, the Philippines, Bali and all over the world. Things continue to get progressively worse because now we even have a new threat from some radical Islamic leaders for individuals to carry out, at will, killings wherever there are crowds of people such as bus stations and shopping centers. We, as a society, are now living on the defensive like never before.

It is not realistic that someday the terrorists will be terminated and that the evil that ravages our land will cease and that the police will all draw early retirement.

The reality is that the world is getting worse, not better. It seems that we are on the brink of a total worldwide financial collapse. Oppressive Sharia law that is diabolically opposed to our constitution and Christian principles is slowly replacing civilization, as we know it around the globe.

The prophecy also tells us in Daniel 12:10 "Many will be purified, made spotless, and refined, but the wicked will continue to be wicked. None of the wicked will understand, but those who are wise will understand." (NIV) A refined life is the good news behind all the suffering. When we make it through we are better people. Sometimes we receive blessings we would not have received without going through the fire of life. So truly the best is yet to come.

The sad part about this scripture is that there are people who are so distracted by the cesspool of wickedness that they will never see the train coming while they are standing on the tracks doing their own evil thing. Part of our battle is to share Christ with people before He returns.

Now do not get me wrong, I am not looking for trouble by any means, even if it means self-improvement. But I believe we grow smarter and wiser through tough times more than we do through the easy times. Even today there are people who are asking deep spiritual questions now that they see Islamic terrorists beheading Christians. People are waking up to the truth that it is all about radical Islam. People are coming to realize that they have been lied to their entire lives concerning the Crusades, Columbus, colonialism, our American forefathers and other redactive history that has been written to fit an agenda that is anti-Christian at its core. The hashtag #WakeUpAmerica on Twitter is going viral, and people in America are waking up and they are angry! The fire has a purifying outcome on a lot of people.

The prophecy continues in Daniel 12:11-12 "From the time that the daily sacrifice is abolished and the abomination that causes desolation is set up, there will be 1,290 days. Blessed is the one who waits for and reaches the end of the 1,335 days."(NIV) Numbers in apocalyptic literature have a more symbolic value than a literal value. Over the years, various people have tried to assign these numbers to specific dates on calendars. Including myself...when the Pope came to speak to Congress in 2015, and we had a 4th blood moon that lined up with some important dates on the Jewish calendar, I thought it was the beginning of the end. Many have made predictions about the end of history and the return of Christ. But nobody has got it right.

And that is because numbers in the Bible are more symbolic than literal. The good news is that God knows and that is the message we are getting from Gabriel, thanks to Michael punching his way through the demonic angels of the territory of Persia. God has an end in mind. It is a mystery to us – but God knows. There will come a time when God, and it is in His timing, will wrap things up.

The good news about these prophecies is that there are only so many days of trouble, and then all this spiritual warfare comes to an end. So this means that perseverance is the name of the game. So keep on fighting the good fight. Do not give up – you may be on the 99th-yard line with one to go. However, only God can see how much yardage there is left to go. We just need to stay fast and fight the evil in the world knowing that in the end we will have the victory!

So, in the midst of the pain, we must trust God and keep on moving the ball down the field. The goal is down there somewhere.

One of my favorite Navy sayings comes from Admiral David Glasgow Farragut. All the highest ranks in the Navy -- rear admiral, vice admiral, and admiral of the Navy -- were created just for this one man. He was the hero of the Battle of Mobile Bay during the

Civil War and other sea encounters. Farragut's rise to the post of admiral in 1866 was the crowning moment in a career that began before he was a teenager and lasted for more than five decades.

The Battle of Mobile Bay had a heavily guarded bay entrance that was filled with mines, then known as torpedoes. Farragut's cry of "Ignore (sic) the torpedoes, full speed ahead!" is not only the stuff of legend, but it was also good tactics. All but one of the fleet's eighteen ships passed safely through the channel, and in August 1864, Mobile Bay's forts fell.[46] That is what this apocalyptic literature is telling us: Ignore the torpedoes, full speed ahead! Move out …get going…the visions and dreams are over…get on with your life.

And do not just move out, go with confidence – the confidence that comes from knowing that God is in control and one day God is going to recall us.

The second half of Daniel 12:13 is extremely important, and it says—

* "You will rest, and then at the end of the days you will rise again to receive your allotted inheritance."(NIV)

We are not going to see it all now, but the inheritance that God has for us will eventually be ours. And we will probably not see it all until the final resurrection.

Let's jump back to Daniel 12:1 –

* "At that time Michael, the archangel who stands guard over your nation, will arise. Then there will be a time of anguish greater than any since nations first came into existence. But at that time every one of your people whose name is written in the book will be rescued."(NLT)

It will be those who put their faith and trust in God who will be preserved, and have their names written in the book of life.

The Apostle Paul in Phil 4:3:
- "Yes, and I ask you, my true companion, help these women since they have contended at my side in the cause of the gospel, along with Clement and the rest of my co-workers, whose names are in the book of life." (NIV)

The Revelation of John in the book of Revelations picks up this theme.

Revelation 3: 5:
- "The one who is victorious will, like them, be dressed in white. I will never blot out the name of that person from the book of life, but will acknowledge that name before my Father and his angels." (NIV)

Revelation 20:15:
- "And anyone whose name was not found recorded in the Book of Life was thrown into the lake of fire."(NLT)

Revelation 21:27:
- "Nothing impure will ever enter it, nor will anyone who does what is shameful or deceitful, but only those whose names are written in the Lamb's book of life." (NIV)

It is not how good you have been; how many little old ladies you have helped across the street; how long you have been sober; how much you did not cheat and steal. But rather it is a matter of putting your trust in the author of the book. And when we do that – when we acknowledge Jesus as Savior and as Master of our lives –Jesus writes you into the story in His book of everlasting life.

Daniel 12:2:

- "Multitudes who sleep in the dust of the earth will awake: some to everlasting life, others to shame and everlasting contempt."(NIV)

The idea of resurrection is not very explicit in the Old Testament – except here in Daniel 12. This is the first clear reference to a resurrection of both the righteous and the wicked in the Bible. This is also the only mention to "eternal life" in the entire Old Testament. It also shows that the choices we make matter because some will have everlasting life and others everlasting contempt.

So, in John 11:25, when Jesus shows up to the grave of Lazarus and proclaims: "I am the resurrection and the life" (NIV), the crowd was hearing these words in the context of this Daniel chapter 12 passage – for this was the most specific reference to resurrection in the scriptures that the Jews had. There is no way Daniel could have possibly seen or understood the whole thing. But this prophecy is foreshadowing the resurrection of Jesus. I do not know about you, but to me this prophecy is an awesome testimony that God is sovereign and in control.

By looking at a snapshot of our final victory over sin and death and receiving a command to go out and live life to the fullest because we know that there is final victory in our future is a great way for us to end this book.

Hear Daniel 12, verse 13 again—

- "As for you, go your way till the end. You will rest, and then at the end of your days, you will rise to receive your allotted inheritance."(NIV)

Resurrection is the good news that the Jewish slaves of sixth century BC needed to hear. And, in actuality, this is what we need to hear today!

There is hope! And it's rooted in the resurrection. All of this brings us back to the key point, which is the key point for the whole book of Daniel. God is in control.

It may look like things are spinning out of control now – but that is only because we lack perspective and because we are not taking the resurrection factor into account of our final victory.

So the book of Daniel gives us the right perspective on how to live in a world full of evil. We all now know what the book of Daniel says. So let's allow it to shape the way we see the world and our response to the challenges that the world throws at us.

Ignore the torpedoes…full speed ahead! Come, Lord Jesus!

What is the bad news?

What is the good news?

Explain the foreshadowing of "everlasting life"?

What does "everlasting life" mean to you?

How does Daniel's view of the resurrection compare to your view of the resurrection?

Is your name written in the book of life?

Explain the sovereign power of God?

"It was pride that changed angels into devils; it is humility that makes men as angels."
--Saint Augustine

Pray this prayer for Humility by John Wesley. I have modernized the original text.

> O Lamb of God, who, both by your example and teaching, instructed us to be meek and humble, give me grace throughout my whole life, in every thought, and word, and work, to imitate your meekness and humility. Crush the whole body of pride in me; grant me to feel that I am nothing and have nothing, and that I deserve nothing but shame and contempt, but misery and punishment. Grant, O Lord, that I may look for nothing, claim nothing; and that I may go through all the scenes of life, not seeking my own glory, but looking wholly unto you, and acting wholly for you.
>
> Let me never speak any word that may tend to my own praise, unless the good of my neighbor requires it; and even then let me beware, lest, to heal another, I wound my own soul. Let my ears and my heart be ever shut to the praise that comes from men.
>
> Give me an alarm of applause; in whatsoever form, and from whatsoever tongue, it comes. Deliver my soul from this

snare of hell; neither let me spread it for the feet of others. Whosoever perishes thereby, let their blood be upon their own head, and let not my hand be upon them.

O giver of every good and perfect gift, if at any time you please to work by my hand, teach me to discern what is my own from what is another's, and to render unto you the things that are yours. As all the good that is done on earth you do it yourself, let me ever return to you all the glory. Let me, as a pure crystal, transmit all the light you pour upon me; but never claim as my own what is your exclusive property. Amen[47]

END NOTES

1   Archangels, Michael & Gabriel -- whyangels?com. (n.d.). Retrieved from http://www.whyangels.com/archangels_michael_gabriel.html

2   Spiritual Warfare - How to Know if You are in a Battle. (n.d.). Retrieved from http://www.biblestudytools.com/bible-study/topical-studies/spiritual-warfare-les

3   John Wesley of Evil Angels

4   deliveranceplace.com. (n.d.). Retrieved from http://www.deliveranceplace.com/dprayers.html

5   Spiritual Warfare - How to Know if You are in a Battle. (n.d.). Retrieved from http://www.biblestudytools.com/bible-study/topical-studies/spiritual-warfare-les

6   (Greek Orthodox Prayer):Other Orthodox Prayers. (n.d.). Retrieved from http://www.orthodoxprayer.org/OtherPrayers.html

7   "embreaking" a word I made up meaning "to start interrupting this world with God's Kingdom"

8   What is the Roman Catholic tradition of exorcism? - Quora. (n.d.). Retrieved from https://www.quora.com/What-is-the-Roman-Catholic-tradition-of-exorcism

9   Difference Between Oppression and Possession | Retrieved from http://www.differencebetween.net/miscellaneous/religion-miscellaneous/difference

10   Orthodox Christian Guardian Angel Prayers. (n.d.). Retrieved from http://angels.about.com/od/AngelsReligiousTexts/f/What-Are-Some-Orthodox-Christi

11   John Wesley Sermon 43 The Scripture Way of Salvation

12   John Wesley Sermon 43 The Scripture Way of Salvation

13   Against the Lustful Desires - ChristiansTT. (n.d.). Retrieved from http://christianstt.com/prayer-against-lustful-desires/

14   Prayer for Protection Against Demonic Oppression | Truth in ... (n.d.). Retrieved from http://truthinreality.com/2012/08/14/prayer-for-protection-against-demonic-oppre

15   Prayer for Protection Against Demonic Oppression | Truth in ... (n.d.). Retrieved from http://truthinreality.com/2012/08/14/prayer-for-protection-against-demonic-oppre

[16] Sermon 72 - Of Evil Angels

[17] Sermon 72 - Of Evil Angels

[18] Sermon 72 - Of Evil Angels.

[19] TodayDivorcedMoms.com | Article. (n.d.).
      Retrieved from http://divorcedmoms.com/articles/
      narssist-the-personality-disorder-you-do-not-wa

[20] http://www.orthodoxprayer.org/OtherPrayers.html

[21] Other Orthodox Prayers. (n.d.). Retrieved from http://www.
      orthodoxprayer.org/OtherPrayers.html

[22] Other Orthodox Prayers. (n.d.). Retrieved from http://www.
      orthodoxprayer.org/OtherPrayers.html

[23] Eight Negative Reasons Pastors Leave a Church - ThomRainer.
      com. (n.d.). Retrieved from http://thomrainer.com/2012/12/
      eight-negative-reasons-pastors-leave-a-church/

[24] m.Yoma 5.13

[25] (n.d.). Retrieved from http://www.catholicprayerbook.net/CQprayers/
      prayerforenemies.htm

[26] OSS Simple Sabotage Manual, Sections 11, 12 - CAcert.org. (n.d.).
      Retrieved from http://svn.cacert.org/CAcert/CAcert_Inc/Board/oss/
      oss_sabotage.html

[27] Orthodox Christian Guardian Angel Prayers. (n.d.). Retrieved
      from http://angels.about.com/od/AngelsReligiousTexts/f/
      What-Are-Some-Orthodox-Christi

[28] 2014Overcoming Mobbing: A Recovery Guide for Workplace
      Aggression ... (n.d.). Retrieved from https://store.kobobooks.com/en-US/
      ebook/overcoming-mobbing-a-recovery-guide-for-

[29] -- Saul Alinsky. Rules for Radicals.

[30] 1972 Vintage Books paperback edition of Rules for Radicals by Saul D.
      Alinksy

[31] Donald Reitzes and Dietrich Reitzes (Summer 1987). "Alinsky in the
      1980s: Two Contemporary Chicago Community Organizations." Midwest
      Sociological Society. 2/28: 265.

[32] Bullying in work groups: The impact of leadership
      (PDF ... (n.d.). Retrieved from http://www.researchgate.net/
      publication/233825159_Bullying_in_work_groups_The_im

[33] From the Alban Weekly - Week of 12/04/2006 - jpduua.org. (n.d.).
      Retrieved from http://jpduua.org/sites/default/files/Twenty%20
      Observations%20About%20Troubled%2

[34] Prayer Listings - Catholic Quiver. (n.d.). Retrieved from http://www.
      catholicprayerbook.net/CQprayers/prayerforenemies.htm

[35] I found these statistics in a submitted paper Forced Termination of
      American Clergy: Its Effects and Connection to Negative Well-Being by
      Marcus N. Tanner, Anisa M. Zvonkovic, Charlie Adams Published online
      December 2011 Copyright Religious Research Organization Inc. 2011

36 Clergy Who Experience Trauma as a Result of Forced ... (n.d.). Retrieved from http://link.springer.com/article/10.1007%2Fs10943-012-9571-3

37 Orthodox Prayers before Bedtime - Orthodox Resources for ... (n.d.). Retrieved from http://www.saintgregoryoutreach.org/2010/10/prayer-before-bedtime.html

38 Loc 259 Wounded by God's People: Discovering How God's Love Heals Our ... (n.d.). Retrieved from http://www.goodreads.com/book/show/17841888-wounded-by-god-s-people

39 http://www.jmm.org.au/articles/8592.htm

40 Managing The Clergy Killer Phenomenon by G. Lloyd Redige. (n.d.). Retrieved from http://listserv.virtueonline.org/pipermail/virtueonline_listserv.virtueon

41 listserv.virtueonline.org, http://listserv.virtueonline.org/pipermail/virtueonline_listserv.virtueonline.or (accessed December 04, 2015).

42 Managing The Clergy Killer Phenomenon by G. Lloyd Redige. (n.d.). Retrieved from http://listserv.virtueonline.org/pipermail/virtueonline_listserv.virtueon

43 Beck, A, Rush, A. John, Shaw, B, Emery, G. Cognitive Therapy of Depression, Guilford Press, 1979
Lazarus, A, Fay, A, I can if I want to, William Morrow Co. 1975
Ellis, Albert and Dryden, Windy. The Practice of Rational Emotive Therapy. Springer Publishing company 1987

44 Thanksgiving After Trouble - serbianchurchstlouis.com. (n.d.). Retrieved from http://www.serbianchurchstlouis.com/files/Thanksgiving_After_Trouble

45 Disney - There's A Great Big Beautiful Tomorrow Lyrics. (n.d.). Retrieved from http://www.songlyrics.com/disney/there-s-a-great-big-beautiful-tomorrow-lyrics/

46 Joining the Military - Military.com. (n.d.). Retrieved from http://www.military.com/Recruiting/Content/0,13898,diversity_davidfarragut,,00.h

47 Prayers for Humility - Knowing Jesus. (n.d.). Retrieved from http://prayer.knowing-jesus.com/Prayers-for-Humility

Contact Mike Mayhugh at www:mayhughbeblessed.com

or

wmmayhugh@yahoo.com

or

Batttle READY with Mayhugh on Facebook

Life Coaching available to Pastors who have been through distress and mobbing.

Limited speaking and seminar opportunities.

Look forward to Mike's next book:

Hell is for Real

Memoirs of what was intended for evil, God used for good.

If you have a story you would like to share to be considered for Hell is for Real please email me your testimony of God's redemption to the above email.

If you would like to share your testimony of how Battle Ready has affected your life or stories of similar conflicts with evil and would like to share for possible use in a second addition of Battle Ready please use the above email.

Printed in the United States
By Bookmasters